DISCOVER CAPE COD

Shawnie Kelley

Enjoy discovering the Cape !

Shawnie

WANDERLUST TRAVEL PRESS

WANDERLUST TRAVEL PRESS
COLUMBUS, OHIO

DISCOVER CAPE COD
1ST EDITION

A Wanderlust Travel Press Book

Copyright © 2016 by Wanderlust Travel Press

Cover design: Sherri Pickett
Cover Map: Walker Lith & Pub Co. Boston 1917
Text Design: Sherri Pickett
Back Cover: *Boats in Nantucket Harbor*, Shawnie Kelley

Photo Credits: See Bibliography and Sources

Library of Congress Cataloging–in–Publication Data
Kelley, Shawnie
Discover Cape Cod/Shawnie Kelley—1st ed.
        Includes bibliographical reference and index.
        ISBN 978–0–9903236–0–0 (pbk); ISBN 978–0–9903236–1–7 (ebook)
        1. Cape Cod (Mass.)—History—Anecdotes.

Manufactured in the United States of America
First Edition/First Printing

DISCOVER CAPE COD

Shawnie Kelley

CONTENTS

CONTENTS

PREFACE

Discover Cape Cod is more than a collection of short historical stories. This book is a history meets travel guide. It is the culmination of years of traveling with a curiosity and passion for the past. Cape Cod is a sensory driven place where knowing the 'who', 'what' and 'why' of this destination helps to create a true sense of place, which can enrich one's travels.

Each story here includes an interactive experience to help bring to life that particular moment in time. It shows the past can be felt with a simple hike through the same terrain the founding fathers trekked or by watching fog roll in to Chatham Beach, remembering all the ships lost in centuries of nor'easters.

I've come to appreciate what Cape Cod represents to different people, so the stories selected for this edition represent a cross-section of topics, towns, and time periods—a little something for everyone. Whether you are a history buff, avid traveler, or general lover of Cape Cod, this book allows you to experience the past while discovering Cape Cod of today.

I hope you enjoy this experiential approach to exploring the Cape.

Shawnie

ACKNOWLEDGMENTS

I would like to recognize several people who helped to bring this history-meets-travel guide to fruition. First, my business partner, travel buddy, and great friend, Sherri Pickett was central to the design and technical aspects of making this book. As a partner in Wanderlust Tours and Wanderlust Travel Press, she and I have collaborated on a variety of professional projects, including *Discover Cape Cod*. We were both excited to create a book that brings together history and travel—two passions that she and I share. I owe Sherri ongoing gratitude for keeping our many projects on task and my word count in check.

I also owe my husband, Kevin Foy, heartfelt thanks for his active involvement: from chauffeuring us around the Cape to using our vacation time to do research. We have enjoyed making new discoveries together through the years, but always look forward to visiting our favorite haunts, like the Dan'l Webster Inn in Sandwich, Baxter's Boat House in Hyannisport, and Chatham Bars Inn.

My mother, Kitty Pollick, and sister, Mandy Jones, have also been invaluable to my writing process. They both have spent plenty of time on Cape Cod and provided honest feedback about each chapter. Sherri's mother, Jackie Pickett, has lent an editorial eye and valuable input to this manuscript. This book is dedicated to you three fabulous ladies.

ACKNOWLEDGMENTS

Lots of family and friends have spent time together with me on the Cape. Some have pointed me to exciting new discoveries, which I find is still possible even after decades of visiting the Cape, while others have just come along for the fun and embraces all that Cape Cod has to offer. Thank you to the Boston Beckwith family, the Pittsburgh Kelley family, the Columbus Foy family, Chet Domitz, Chaya Chandrasekhar, Andrew Lamoreaux, Andy VerHage, and Julie Allodi—your gift of the Nantucket hooked rug still adorns the sunroom. We would also like to thank Sherri's husband Dan and her stepchildren—Carolyn, Alisa, Andrew, and Jason for their tireless support.

Finally, I'm sending up a huge thank you en masse to all of the nice people at the various historical societies, museums, visitor centers, Edible Cape Cod, Truro Winery, Cape Cod National Seashore, and Cape Cod Community College. Thanks to those of you who took time to respond to emails, phone calls, answer questions, and fill requests for information. Some of my best "research" involved countless hours of chatting up locals and travelers at restaurants, bars, stores, markets, and marinas all around the Cape. The wealth of interesting stories that were shared with me could fill several volumes.

The maps within this book have been reprinted with permission of the Cape Cod Chamber of Commerce. Also greatly appreciated are the usage rights for many of the images reproduced throughout the book. We have done due diligence to locate the original sources of all of the images, however if any of the pictures are not accurately credited, please contact Wanderlust Travel Press via email at info@wanderlusttravelpress.com.

To participate in the ongoing discoveries and conversations about Cape Cod, join our fans on Facebook (DiscoverCapeCod), Instagram (discovercapecod), and Twitter (@DiscoverCapeCod) or sign up for our monthly newsletter at Wanderlust-Tours.com.

INTRODUCTION

Cape Cod is the bared and bended arm of Massachusetts: the shoulder is at Buzzard's Bay; the elbow, or crazy–bone is at Cape Mallebarre [Chatham]; the wrist at Truro; and the sandy fist at Provincetown ... boxing with northeast storms, and, ever and anon, heaving her Atlantic adversary from the lap of the earth

—Henry David Thoreau

Between 1849 and 1857, the author, poet, and naturalist, Henry David Thoreau spent several weeks walking the "bared and bended arm of Massachusetts," absorbing its atmosphere, visiting most of its towns, while recording his thoughts, which culminated in to his 1865 publication of *Cape Cod*. The imagery filling Thoreau's memoirs are the same images that come to mind 150 years later: sandy dunes covered with billowing grass, tall ships sunken in icy nor'easters, and the moody Atlantic Ocean battering seaside shanties. He was visionary enough to recognize the powerful appeal and thought–provoking nature of the Cape. Thoreau predicted this coast would be a place of resort for those who truly wished to experience the seaside—and he was right.

Today, tourism is the Cape's number one industry, attracting 1.3 million visitors annually. But Thoreau's contagious reverence for solitude and natural history is not

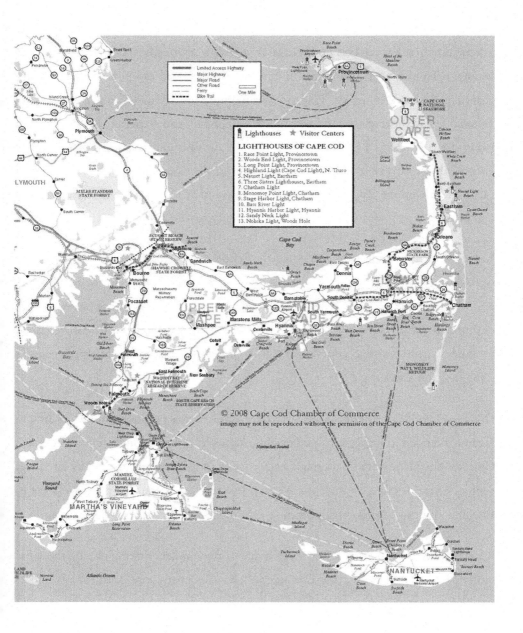

lost on those of us living in the fast–paced twenty–first century. People continue to flock to Cape Cod and the islands in search of peace and tranquility, history and folklore, shipwrecks and ghost stories. Some folk are fascinated with the Cape for its colonial and maritime history; some are smitten with its bounty of seafood, while others just come for the beaches. Whatever your reasons, nearly 400 years of American history permeate every nook and cranny of every harbor and beach. *Discover Cape Cod* helps you to explore the Cape in a way where history meets experiential travel. Twenty-seven short stories are enhanced with hands–on experiences, which help bring the past to life. The book also includes a bit of bonus trivia and a brief travel compendium covering some basics for visiting the Cape, Martha's Vineyard, and Nantucket. *Discover Cape Cod* proves there is so much more to Massachusetts' bared and bended arm than just beautiful beaches and great seafood.

Learn of legendary pilgrims and notorious pirates who pervade Cape Cod's popular history, and also of the unfamiliar artists, poets, entrepreneurs, inventors, and worldly sea captains who left an equally indelible mark. Here are tales of people who have endured isolation, survived wars, weathered storms, and made, lost, and regained fortunes within a single generation. These are stories of remarkable perseverance, struggles, and successes.

Discover Cape Cod introduces Captain Mayo, a Brewster sea captain who, according to legend, intended to smuggle Napoleon to America. We take you in search of Jeremiah's Gutter—the Cape's first man–made canal. Some of the other stories focus on "firsts," such as America's first transatlantic wireless telegraph message sent from Wellfleet to England and the Cape's first lighthouse, commissioned by George Washington.

"Graveyard of the Atlantic" tells the eerie tale of two tankers sinking during the same violent storm, thus prompting the biggest Coast Guard rescue in history. While in

INTRODUCTION

Chatham, it's difficult not to reflect on this bittersweet tragedy once you realize the stern of one of the ships rests just beyond the bar near Monomoy. "An Island for Fair Martha" encourages us to remember the young child for whom the vineyard is named, while a pilgrimage to Wellfleet or Provincetown is enriched after reading "Legend of the Whydah" and "Ghost Ship Rising"—two stories about the illustrious "Pirate Prince," "Black Sam" Bellamy and his sunken treasure recovered by a dreamer who believed in it.

Every town on the Cape has a fascinating history and a wealth of interesting stories all worthy of inclusion here, but *Discover Cape Cod* shares only a small cross–section of important military, maritime, scientific, and economic events that have shaped the development of the Cape, while integrating unique ways to experience it. Native American history certainly pre–dates the English settlements and there are plenty of Indian monuments and sites to visit around Cape Cod, but the stories here begin with the European colonization of the Cape since reliable written sources are more readily available.

Drawing on firsthand accounts, newspaper articles, historical documents, and decades of traveling the Cape, author and Wanderlust Tours owner, Shawnie Kelley takes readers on a journey through 400 years of Cape Cod history in a collection of 27 short stories. Each historical tale is further enhanced with thoughtful suggestions on how to experience this moment in time: whether it's hiking through legendary landscape, visiting a museum or historic landmark, seeking out a bucolic beach or indulging in classic Cape Cod cuisine.

Cape Cod is historic. Cape Cod is experiential. And this book brings the two together in ways that make discovering Cape Cod a rich, educational travel experience.

1

AN ISLAND FOR
FAIR MARTHA

MARTHA'S VINEYARD
− 1602 −

When compared with the French, Spanish, and Dutch, the English were slow to take interest in colonizing North America, but by the late sixteenth century an enterprising group of Englishmen from Suffolk began to consider permanently settling in The New World.

Lawyer, explorer, and privateer, Captain Bartholomew Gosnold was instrumental in establishing the first permanent settlement in Jamestown, Virginia. While leading the prospecting expedition to Virginia, their ship skirted the coastline of what would soon become known as New England. During this historic voyage, many of Cape Cod's significant landmarks were named. The exploration of this region is documented in the journal of Gabriel Archer, one of Gosnold's travel companions.

On March 26, 1602, Bartholomew Gosnold and his crew boarded their barque and set sail from Falmouth, England, for the New World. Aboard the *Concord* was a group of colonists, including eight mariners and twenty–three gentlemen adventurers. A few eventually returned to England and published tales of their discoveries, which helped promote the colonization of Cape Cod.

In early May, the Labrador Current was pushing the rugged, 50–foot vessel southward along the coast of Maine and Massachusetts. The men were clearly fascinated with the diversity of birds for which they had no name in their English tongue. By May 14, the crew caught the first glimpse of land, which is believed to have been the headland of Massachusetts' other, more northerly, peninsula of Cape Ann.

After dropping anchor, Gosnold extended his spyglass for a look around and quickly spotted a small boat carrying what he believed to be "distressed Christians" toward their ship. As the shallop drew closer, the crew was surprised to see it contained eight curious Indians, who were even more curiously dressed in European breeches and waistcoats.

The visitors came in peace. Much to Gosnold's surprise, the welcoming committee was able to speak French, Spanish, and Portuguese words. Gabriel Archer noticed that the Indians understood their English much better than the Englishmen understood the native tongue. Gosnold's men were by no means the first tourists to pass through Cape Cod. It was unbeknownst to them that the North American coast had for hundreds of years prior been the site of summer camps for Portuguese, Basque, and Scandinavian fishermen. The Native Americans had sustained contact with "white men" for a very long time.

After friendly exchanges with the Indians, the crew decided to press on to their final destination in Virginia. Gosnold thanked the locals for pointing them in the right direction, named the jetty of land "Savage Rock", and "set sail westward, leaving them and their coast."

A short time later, the Concord sailed into the waters of Cape Cod where the crew once again sighted land. They initially believed the Cape to be an island because of the great gulf of water lying westward of it. The Captain chose to name this large sound "Shoal Hope" for its shallow waters and hazardous sandy bottom.

It was somewhere along the Lower Cape, near present–day Truro or Wellfleet, where they dropped anchor and sent a group of men ashore to see what the "island" had to offer. They found the land full of unripe strawberries, birch trees, and deep sand dunes. Another friendly Indian lent them a helping hand in navigating the terrain, but the explorers returned to the ship at nightfall with little to report.

Those who stayed on board the ship during the day bragged that the fishing along the Atlantic coast was at least as good as that in Newfoundland. In fact, the men had caught so many fish they had to throw a countless number back into the sea. Having taken a "great store of codfish," Gosnold decided to change the bay's name from Shoal Hope to Cape Cod—and the name stuck.

The following morning, the Concord sailed a little farther along the coast, then dropped anchor near a sandy beach so another expedition could go exploring. After hiking up the highest of hills, they realized this piece of land was not at all an island, but a mile–wide, sandy peninsula separated from the mainland by the great Cape Cod Bay.

Having gained his bearings, the captain continued maneuvering the ship through hazardous shoals along the entire length of the outer coast of the Cape, eventually landing near present–day Woods Hole in Falmouth. Standing on the buggy beach, Bartholomew Gosnold gazed out over the water and, like thousands of modern–day travelers do each summer, headed for the big island seven miles off in the distance.

The sprawling island seemed uninhabited, but the Englishmen were unaware this place called Noepe—or "dry place amid waters"—was home to Wampanoag Indians for thousands of years. Gosnold's arrival marked the beginning of the Vineyard's European history and the decline of the Wampanoags.

The men went ashore on the morning of May 22, 1602 and finding this new island extremely pleasant, decided to spend the night. Gabriel Archer wrote admiringly of the rolling landscape and local nature. They found cranes and geese and took in an even larger store of codfish than they had earlier in the bay.

After collecting a great haul of cod, the Concord doubled back around the west end of the Vineyard, sailing past the sweeping clay cliffs of present–day Aquinnah. The Englishmen were reminded of the chalky cliffs along the coastline of southern England and initially dubbed this distinct headland Dover Cliffs, but by 1662, sailors changed its name to "Gayhead," because of the gaily–colored striations in the earth. Gayhead was eventually split into two words—Gay Head—and remained so named until 1997 when the city voted to revert back to its original Indian name, 'Aquinnah' meaning, "land under the hill."

The serene wooded terrain covered with wild grape vines prompted Gosnold to name the beautiful island Martha's Vineyard after his one–year–old daughter who had died a few years earlier. At Bury St. Edmonds in eastern England, where young Martha is buried, the original gravestone marking her place of rest no longer exists; but her short life was immortalized in the naming of one of America's most popular holiday spots.

EXPERIENCE

Do what Gosnold did and circumnavigate Martha's Vineyard (by car, bus or bicycle). It's easy to hit a number of villages in a day trip, but try to spend a few nights on the island to make the most of a Martha's Vineyard experience. Ferries leaving Falmouth or Hyannisport dock either at Vineyard Haven or Oak Bluffs.

If you land in Vineyard Haven, stock up on Black Dog gear from the general store and have a wonderful meal at the Art Cliff Diner. Arriving in Oak Bluffs puts you within easy walking or biking distance of the famed 130–year old East Chop Lighthouse with its wonderful views from lookout point. Oak Bluffs, nicknamed "Cottage City" for its 200 eclectic, colorful Victorian cottages, is also home to America's oldest operating platform carousel, *The Flying Horses Carousel.*

When visiting the genteel village of Edgartown, make sure to stop for a photo –op at the American Legion Memorial Bridge—the wooden bridge made famous in the movie Jaws and where throngs of people continue to take the (albeit illegal) plunge into the churning waters. Martha's Vineyard Museum in Edgartown is a great place to dig deep in to Vineyard history. Its ambitious exhibitions offer an overview of the entire recorded history of the Enchanted Isle. Immerse yourself in the bygone days of this former whaling town with a leisurely wander through charming streets lined with traditional architecture, art galleries, and interesting old churches. While walking, look upward to see many of the home's topped with a 'widow's walk'—a fenced rooftop deck from which women would watch for their husband's ships to, hopefully, return safely to port.

Plan ahead to grab a two minute ferry ride from Edgartown out to Chappaquiddick Island. The *On Time II* and *On Time III* ferries carry bike–toting picnickers a mere 527 feet out to Chappy, as the locals call it. There's not much happening on this slender finger of sandy land and cars are not recommended, but this sort of excursion is an easy escape from the Vineyard crowds, which can be elbow–to–elbow through the summer. Chappy is one of the quietest spots on the Vineyard.

Driving the length of Martha's Vineyard without traffic takes about 20 minutes. Spend a few hours on the windswept west end of the island around Aquinnah for some peace and tranquility. Hike from Gay Head Lighthouse down to Moshup's Beach (named for the Wampanoag god who created the island)—a hauntingly beautiful and occasionally desolate part of the Vineyard, at least during off–season. Here you get close up perspectives of the striking cliffs that caught Bartholomew Gosnold's eye. But be warned, you may get an eyeful, as the cove–like beaches attract sunbathers who often strip down to nothing. Finally, don't miss the 150–year old Gay Head Lighthouse, which stands only 46 feet from a drastically eroding cliff. Plans are in motion to physically relocate the building in an attempt to preserve this island treasure; an effort similar to the moving of Truro's Highland Lighthouse, a story told later in the book.

2

GOSNOLD'S HOPE & ELIZABETH'S ISLE

CUTTYHUNK ISLAND
– 1602 –

In 1602, Elizabeth I was Queen of England. Her reign marked an age of adventure; a time during which North America was extensively explored and mapped by the French, Spanish, and English. Claiming and naming a new land for one's monarch was the modus operandi for most European explorers. Englishman Bartholomew Gosnold went astray of protocol by naming the first island he discovered in the New World after his daughter, Martha, but he didn't forget about his queen.

In late May Gosnold and his crew spent three days exploring Martha's Vineyard. They admired the island, appreciated its bounty of wild grape vines, and considered it safe, but decided to keep moving. The goal was, after all, to settle in Virginia. The ship sailed through the night, making its way around Gayhead Cliffs through Vineyard Sound. By morning, Gosnold's expedition entered the choppy waters of Buzzards Bay, a body of water that is now linked to Cape Cod Bay by the canal. Gabriel Archer was smitten with the scenery enough to write that it was "one of the stateliest sounds ever I was in. This we called Gosnold's Hope."

The explorers found a chain of islands stretching from present–day Woods Hole in Falmouth to Rhode Island Sound, separating Vineyard Sound from Buzzards Bay. Gosnold's expedition created a permanent settlement on the most westerly of these islands, which they named in honor of their queen. He believed Elizabeth Island would be a great location for a trading post.

The small island, situated only 14 miles off the coast of the present–day city of New Bedford, was minimally inhabited by natives who hunted and fished on these islands, but did not reside here year–round. This gave the group a feeling of safety, which added to the island's appeal. They were also quick to find a good supply of wood and a source of fresh water—a commodity not readily available on the main lands of Cape Cod.

Gosnold instructed several men to construct a rustic fort near a freshwater pond, which would serve as a base of operations while Gosnold and a few others went out investigating the island. During the week, the men at the base camp collected sassafras, sowed grain seeds, and made a flat–bottomed boat called a punt, for easy maneuvering over the marshy ponds.

Gosnold's expedition returned a few days later with a canoe that had been left behind by local Indians then set off to survey the mainland near New Bedford. Upon their return to the fort, Gosnold showed off quite a haul of gifts: furs, turtles, and hemp given to them by the courteous and attractive people on the "goodliest continent he had ever seen." He knew this region was ripe for international trade, and the island's location was ideal for a trading post.

Gosnold mustered up an ambitious plan to leave twenty men behind to establish a trading–post, while the rest would return with him to Great Britain to secure and bring back more provisions. Before setting sail for England, the men set to building a more fortified fort – a buzz of activity that piqued the Wampanoags' interest.

While most of the crew were aboard the ship, a group of fifty natives equipped with bows and arrows arrived on the island. There were only eight men in the camp at the time, including Gabriel Archer, who thought to approach the Indians with his musket and gesture to them with an option of peace or war. The Indians had come in peace and the groups sat down together.

Captain Gosnold made his way from the boat to the island with twelve others. He was greeted as the leader of the English group and gave the Indian chief a straw hat, which he immediately put on, along with a set of forged knives, at which they marveled. It was this courtesy that Archer claims "made them all fall in love with us."

After a rainy day forced everyone aboard the ship, they were finally able to get back to work in early June. The curious Chief and his men came around again and this time, were invited to stay for dinner. Apparently, drinks flowed and the spirited group had a good laugh at the Indian's reaction to the unfamiliar piquancy of mustard seasoning stinging their nostrils. The environment was relaxed and relations seemed good with the locals.

The eighth of June was the day of reckoning. Supplies were to be divided up between the ship and the fort—and it didn't take long for controversy to arise. The twenty men staying behind to man the trading post claimed that only six weeks of supplies had been issued for what might be up to a six–month wait for fresh provisions. There were whispers of Captain Gosnold pilfering the goods for himself while in England – or perhaps, not returning at all.

Compromises were eventually struck, with nine chosen to stay on Elizabeth Island to finish building the storehouse. Captain Gosnold took the *Concord* and sailed off in search of firewood to shore up their surplus as a gesture of good faith. Those holding down the fort were left with only three meals and a promise Gosnold would return the next day. While he was gone, more Indians paid yet another visit out of uneasy curiosity. This, coupled with a sneaking suspicion that they might have been stranded, left the settlers feeling even more uncertain about staying behind.

A full day passed and there was no sign of the ship. Having eaten their rations of food, the men had to find a way to sustain themselves. Against their better judgment, they split up to find food. Later that evening, one group was assaulted by Indians and spent the stormy night hiding out, lost in the thick brush. The next morning, the two groups were joyously reunited, alive but without food—and there was still no sign of Captain Gosnold.

Terror struck at their hearts. Men who were, just the day before, resolute about making this the first permanent English settlement in the New World now spoke of revolt. When hope was fading away with the sun, Gabriel Archer and the others finally heard the captain summon them from off shore. They were relieved. In the end, the group determined that they simply did not have enough provisions to sustain both the ship and a colony. On June 18, 1602, all thirty–two explorers boarded the *Concord* and returned to England, arriving in Exmouth in July.

Elizabeth Island remained an English territory and became a landmark for future sailors, but all that exists of Gosnold's attempted settlement is a sixty–foot monument made of native boulders marking the site of the original fortress. Elizabeth Island is even rumored to have served as the setting for William Shakespeare's play, *The Tempest*. The great bard, who happened to be patronized by the island's namesake, Queen Elizabeth I, might have had access to Gosnold's travel journals or come across one of the voyager's publications. It's an interesting thought that this tiny, obscure New World island might have been immortalized in a famous piece of Renaissance literature.

The colony didn't turn out the way Gosnold had planned, but Elizabeth Island—presently known by its Indian name, Cuttyhunk—remains settled to this day. The town of Gosnold commemorates its English founder.

EXPERIENCE

Between June and September, pack a picnic, grab your bike, and hitch a ferry ride out to Cuttyhunk for an afternoon of solitude in one of the Cape's most bucolic settings. The southernmost of the Elizabeth Islands is barely two miles long and less than a mile wide, so there's absolutely no need for a car. With just a quick bike ride or short hike to the center of the island, you are rewarded with sweeping views of Vineyard Sound from Lookout Hill. Don't miss a visit to Gosnold's Monument and the pretty nature hikes around the ponds. The trails are easily navigable, but pay attention to the private property signs.

The Fish Market at the Town Dock serves limited (but always excellent) seafood during a small window around lunchtime. You'll find public restrooms and fishing charters here too. Cuttyhunk's practically non–existent little village has one café, general store, ice cream stall, and the occasional food cart. So, come prepared. One daily round trip ferry service is provided by the M/V Cuttyhunk between New Bedford's Fisherman's Wharf and the island, so don't miss your return ferry, as spontaneous lodging options are slim pickings. The year round ferry schedule is online at *www.cuttyhunkferryco.com*, while everything else you need to know about Cuttyhunk can be found on the island's official website: *www.cuttyhunk.net*.

3

CHAMPLAIN'S KETTLE CONTROVERSY

ORLEANS

− 1605 −

LANDING OF THE PILGRIMS AT PLYMOUTH 11ᵗʰ DEC.1620.

Samuel de Champlain was a seventeenth–century French explorer and skillful navigator who mapped and claimed much of northeastern North America for King Henry IV of France. As "geographer royal," Champlain developed a pattern of exploring and mapping a region for several months, then returning to France to relay his discoveries to the king and acquire more funding. He made at least twenty Atlantic crossings in his lifetime; driven by an intense desire to "obtain a knowledge of different countries, regions and realms."

In 1603, Champlain was sent to New France (present–day Canada and Maine), to further Jacques Cartier's discoveries from a half–century earlier. He first sailed around Cape Cod and Martha's Vineyard in 1604, then again in 1605 and 1606. During the latter two visits Champlain surveyed the coastline; drawing up what historians consider the oldest recognizable map of what is now New England. His map refers to Cape Cod as Cap Blanc, or "the white cape," so named because of its light–colored sand. Apparently, he was unaware or perhaps, just ignoring the fact that Bartholomew Gosnold had named the bay "Cape Cod" a few years earlier.

Champlain was, by no means, the first European to have made contact with the local Natives, but few earlier written accounts exist, all of which are from the "white man's" perspective. One of the earliest mentions of Cape Cod is by the Italian explorer Giovanni da Verrazzano, who investigated many places along the Atlantic coast during his 1524 expedition. Verrazzano mapped his voyages and named many of these places in letters to King Francis I of France. It's also likely the English–funded explorer, John Cabot, encountered Cape Cod on his way to somewhere else.

Samuel de Champlain, however, spent three and a half years carefully charting the coastline and observing the inhabitants between Nova Scotia and Cape Cod. He commented in his journal that all previous descriptions of Cape Cod offered very little in comparison to his own. It is not surprising then, that Champlain provided the first detailed account of high crime on Cape Cod.

Champlain, an incessant journal–keeper, published a story of his travels between the years of 1604 and 1612 in a book titled, *The Voyages of Sieur de Champlain*. He believed that he did his duty as best he could to document everything he saw in greater detail than anyone had before him. His tale of a violent skirmish over a kettle is the first known written documentation of theft and murder on Cape Cod.

In the spring of 1605, Pierre du Gua, the French governor of Acadia rallied a group of colonists to leave St. Croix Island, near Maine, and go in search of a new place to settle. Champlain was traveling as the ship's cartographer, mapping the coast from Maine to Massachusetts during the southward journey from New France.

Along the way, the colonists–to–be made friends with some of the local Indians, visited their villages, and even allowed some of the Wampanoags to join the crew. But Champlain began to lose his trust and admiration for the locals after several conflicts, one of which resulted in the death of a crew member.

The ship dropped anchor in present–day Nauset Harbor in Orleans. A few of the crew went ashore in search of fresh water. After just a few minutes, they came running back to the ship, screaming in French for their mates to open fire on the Indians who were chasing them.

Sure enough, there were several Wampanoags in close pursuit, with weapons in hand. Despite the language barrier, the Wampanoags on the ship could tell there was trouble. All but one, who was detained, leaped overboard into the water, fearing for their safety.

By the time the sailors aboard the ship loaded their muskets, a Wampanoag had shot one of the fleeing men in the back with an arrow, killing him. The musketeers began firing at the Indians from the ship, scaring them off into the woods. Their efforts were too little, too late. All they could do was retrieve their dead crew member and try to figure out what went wrong.

Champlain wrote in his journal that one of the Indians had stolen the kettle in which the sailors planned to carry fresh water back to the ship. A chase ensued, but the Indians were too swift for the Frenchmen. It is unclear how the pursuit turned against the sailors, but there is little doubt the theft escalated into an all—out skir-mish—resulting in the first murder on Cape Cod.

Later that day a group of Wampanoags visited the boat with their leader to reconcile the matter, blaming the theft on another tribe. The Frenchmen released the captive Indian and made peace. From that point on, Champlain claimed the Wampanoags were not to be trusted. "They are great thieves," he wrote, "and, if they cannot lay hold of any thing with their hands, they try to do so with their feet…It is necessary to be on one's guard against this people, and live in a state of distrust with them, yet without letting them perceive it."

There is no written account of this situation from the Native American perspective. Maybe the locals were already feeling encroached upon or had prior bad experiences with the "white man." Maybe the sailors provoked the Indians. There is also the possibility that the Indians did steal the kettle. No one knows for sure the truth of the matter—except perhaps, the dead man.

This story is just one example of how cultural misunderstandings, language barriers, and, quite often, the Europeans' ill—considered actions ignited confrontations with the local Indians. It is hard to say with any certainty the accuracy of Champlain's words or to pinpoint what really instigated the trouble, but it is safe to assume the Natives had experienced both gracious and hostile white men by the time Champlain arrived.

These stories of conflict were often used by the early colonials to define the natives as "savages," and, whether exaggerated or not, they have carried over into popular history. Fifteen years after Champlain's brush with the local Indians, the British pilgrims had their own theft—related experience with the Wampanoags—only this time the Indians weren't the culprits. Read more about this conflict in the later story, *First Encounters.*

EXPERIENCE

Of course, no visit to the Cape is complete without chowing a few bowls of chowdah! While the English colonists may have whipped up kettles of pottage – a hearty stew of potatoes, corn, herbs, and meat—one has to wonder if debates were held over who made the best pottage in the settlement. One might wonder if they appropriated their recipes from the indigenous people who for centuries had been whipping up their own shellfish stews. The same discussion swirls about who serves up the tastiest or most original clam chowder on the Cape. Through the years, my odyssey–de–chowder has amounted to the consumption of countless kettles of soup. A taste for clam chowder is personal, but the consensus is that no one wants mushy potatoes or rubbery clams. We also recognize that the atmosphere in which you dine is almost as important as how good the food tastes! The short list here is compiled from personal experiences, conversations with locals, and social media and online research. Hopefully, the suggestions below, ranging from iconic eateries to seafood shacks around the Cape, prove you are never too far from a good kettle of chowdah.

CHAMPLAIN'S KETTLE CONTROVERSY

UPPER CAPE

Cook's Seafood: 7 Ryan's Way, Mashpee
Falmouth Fish Market: 157 Teaticket Highway, Falmouth
Marshland Restaurant: 109 Route 6A, Sandwich

MID CAPE

Black Cat Tavern: 165 Ocean Street, Hyannis
Captain Parker's Pub: 668 Main Street/Route 28, West Yarmouth
The Dolphin Restaurant: 3250 Main Street, Barnstable Village
The Oyster Co Raw & Grille: 202 Depot Street, Dennis Port
The Skipper: 152 South Shore Drive, South Yarmouth
Wimpy's Seafood Café and Market, 752 Main Street, Osterville

OUTER CAPE

Cobie's: 3260 Main Street, Brewster
George's Fish Market: 30 Kildee Road, Harwich Port
Land Ho! 38 Main Street, Orleans
The Squire: 487 Main Street, Chatham

LOWER CAPE

Arnold's Lobster & Clam Bar: 3580 Route 6, Eastham
Lobster Pot: 321 Commercial Street, Provincetown
Mac's Market, 14D Truro Center Road, Truro (Original market in Wellfleet)
Moby Dick's, 3225 State Highway 6, Wellfleet
Wellfleet Oyster & Bookstore Restaurant: 50 Kendrick Avenue, Wellfleet

MARTHA'S VINEYARD

Martha's Vineyard Chowder Company, 9 Oak Bluffs Avenue, Oak Bluffs

NANTUCKET

The SeaGrille Restaurant, 45 Sparks Avenue (mid–Island), Nantucket

4

THE MAYFLOWER
COMPACT

PROVINCETOWN
– 1620 –

The Mayflower Compact is believed to be one of the earliest examples of democracy in America. It was written on November 11, 1620, by William Bradford, one of the pilgrims aboard the *Mayflower*, a ship bound for Virginia to establish a private permanent colony. These early English settlers brought with them strong religious beliefs and social traditions that set the tone for America's first government.

During the reign of King James I (1603–1625), a puritanical religious group chose to separate itself from the Church of England. Religious upheaval and persecution caused these "Separatists" to leave the Nottinghamshire area of England for the more religiously tolerant country of the Netherlands. Here, they hoped to find religious freedom to live their lives in accordance with their strict beliefs. But, that didn't happen.

The Pilgrims worshiped briefly in Amsterdam, then moved to a congregation in Leiden, where they remained for ten years. A very poor quality of life, combined with looming religious persecution and the potential loss of their children's English identity, were the motivating factors for relocating to the British colony of Virginia.

While in Holland, the Pilgrims purchased a ship called the *Speedwell* in which they returned to England in May of 1620. There, they made contact with the owner of a sizable cargo ship called the *Mayflower*, which was chartered by several merchants in search of financial gain in the New World. The groups were given permission to settle in Northern Virginia—currently the New York Hudson River area. In August 1620, the two ships met up in Southampton, England, and set sail for America.

During the first attempt to make a crossing, the *Speedwell* leaked so badly, it was forced to return to England. The Separatists cut their losses, selling the *Speedwell* and crowding 102 passengers onto the *Mayflower* to brave the Atlantic in one ship. The group included British merchants, skilled craftsmen, hired colonists, and people from the Leiden congregation. Those in search of religious freedom were nicknamed "Saints" while those seeking business opportunities were referred to as "Strangers. Two centuries passed before these early settlers were collectively referred to as Pilgrims.

The Saints and Strangers boarded the *Mayflower* on September 6, 1620, and departed from Plymouth, England, for a second attempt to journey to the New World. According to the only two existing accounts of the voyage, they spent two months crossing treacherous seas in a crowded, disease–infested ship. Words of mutiny were not uncommon.

When land was finally sighted on November 9, the crew of the *Mayflower* realized they were in Cape Cod, well north of Virginia. After a few attempts to push on along the coast, they determined the weather was too rough to risk traveling south. On the cold morning of November 11, 1620, the *Mayflower* dropped anchor in a protected harbor on the tip of Cape Cod, near the Indian site of Paomet, modern–day Provincetown.

Some of the Saints were unhappy with the decision to stay in Cape Cod because they did not have England's permission to settle the area, while a few of the Strangers argued they were no longer bound by contract to the stockholders. Rebellion was brewing. Mindful of the failed settlement in Jamestown, Virginia, just a few years earlier, the Pilgrims agreed they would not make the same mistake. The group understood the need for strong leadership and centralized management, so they created a document that would establish a temporary government until they could get permission from England to colonize the area.

This short contract, called the Mayflower Compact, had long–term results and reads as follows:

> *Agreement Between the Settlers at New Plymouth: 1620 IN THE NAME OF GOD, AMEN. We, whose names are underwritten, the Loyal Subjects of our dread Sovereign Lord King James, by the Grace of God, of Great Britain, France, and Ireland, King, Defender of the Faith, etc. Having undertaken for the Glory of God, and Advancement of the*

Christian Faith, and the Honour of our King and Country, a voyage to plant the first Colony in the northern Parts of Virginia; Do by these presents, solemnly and mutually, in the Presence of God and one another, covenant and combine ourselves together into a civil Body Politick, for our better Ordering and Preservation, and Furtherance of the Ends aforesaid: And by Virtue hereof do enact, constitute, and frame, such just and equal Laws, Ordinances, Acts, Constitutions, and Officers, from time to time, as shall be thought most meet and convenient for the general Good of the Colony; unto which we promise all due Submission and Obedience.

IN WITNESS whereof we have hereunto subscribed our names at Cape–Cod the eleventh of November, in the Reign of our Sovereign Lord King James, of England, France, and Ireland, the eighteenth, and of Scotland the fifty–fourth, Anno Domini; 1620.

While most historians agree the Mayflower Compact was not a constitution in the sense of being a fundamental framework of government, its importance lies in the Pilgrims' firm belief that government was a covenant between men. In order for a government to be legitimate, it had to be recognized and consented to by those it intended to govern. The Pilgrims chose to govern themselves according to the will of the majority.

On November 11, 1620, forty–one men boarded the *Mayflower* and signed an agreement that created a "government of the people, by the people, and for the people," and established the basis for America's first written laws.

EXPERIENCE

Climb 116 steps to the top of Pilgrim Memorial in Provincetown for outstanding views over the sandy fist of Cape Cod. The campanile style tower – inspired by the Torre del Mangia in Siena, Italy—rises 252 feet, making this the tallest all–granite structure in the United States. Descendants of the pilgrims funded the memorial, the U.S. Army Corps of Engineers constructed it, and President Theodore Roosevelt spoke at the laying of the cornerstone on August 20, 1907.

After getting the lay of the land, fortify with creative American and Italian fare at one of P'Town's oldest restaurants, Front Street, located nearby at 230 Commercial Street. Save room for a traditional pastry from the Portuguese Bakery, just up the street—a reminder that the pilgrims weren't the first Europeans to sail into Cape Cod. For hundreds of years, Portuguese fishermen have found their way across the Atlantic onto the eastern shores of North America. The bakery has been serving up a tasty bite of heritage with forty traditional pastries from Portugal and the Azores for more than a hundred years. Nibble on history while wandering the colorful side streets of Provincetown.

5

IN THE FOOTSTEPS
OF PILGRIMS

The Pilgrims first dropped anchor on the sandy, desolate tip of Cape Cod near present-day Provincetown—not in Plymouth as popular history teaches us. Firsthand accounts of the earliest explorations of these settlers are offered in writing by two men who made the crossing, William Bradford and Edward Winslow. The presence of these English pioneers is felt and seen in historic monuments all over the northern neck of Cape Cod. The plaques at Pilgrim's Spring and Corn Hill in Truro commemorate two of the first places they made their mark.

After signing the Mayflower Compact on Saturday, November 11, 1620, the Pilgrims began exploring the area they were planning to call home. Saints and Strangers alike were well aware that they had landed in Cape Cod, and that their charter did not permit settlement of the region north of what is now New York City. But since the icy winter would soon be settling in, they chose not to travel any farther south, and sought an official charter to create a colony in New England.

Sixteen men went ashore in a shallop, or small boat, to seek out a place where they could settle and build their new colony. The group was greeted by rolling hills and moors that must have been vaguely reminiscent of their homeland. Taking a quick look around, the men found sandy dunes, juniper trees, and wild grass that ran all the way down to the water in some places—but not much else. With firewood in hand, the party returned to the ship at nightfall and reported having seen no person and no sign of habitation, only marshy ponds and thousands of birds.

The next day, everyone remained on the *Mayflower* in honor of the Sabbath, during which they offered up prayers of thanksgiving for their safe arrival. The following two days were spent bringing the women and children ashore. The carpenters set to work repairing their badly damaged shallop, while the women, under adequate guard, did laundry, and the kids ran off two months' worth of pent-up energy.

Significant scouting expeditions, or "discoveries," along the coastline around present-day Truro began on Wednesday, November 15, 1620, and are described in full in a document titled *Mourt's Relations*. Captain Myles Standish, William Bradford,

Stephen Hopkins, and Edward Tilley, along with twelve others, began exploring the narrow, northern neck of Cape Cod on foot.

It was this same day the search party first sighted the locals, but the six natives and their dog quickly vanished into the forest as the group approached. After pursuing the locals to no avail, the men camped on the beach for the night.

Unable to locate the Indians the following day, the party refocused their energy to finding fresh drinking water. After wandering through miles of thick underbrush, they came upon a fresh-water spring in a clearing at the bottom of a hill. The words on a modern-day plaque at Pilgrim's Spring are taken from firsthand accounts: "about ten o'clock we came into a deepe valley brush, wood-gaille and long grass, through which we found little paths or tracks and there we saw a deere and found springs of fresh water of which we were heartily glad and sat us downe and drunke our first New England water." Edward Winslow, a member of the expedition, wrote that they drank "with as much delight as ever we drunk drink in all our lives."

Rejuvenated, the men pressed on through the small hills, and later that day they came upon mounds of sand that they thought to be Indian graves. The heaps seemed so newly formed that they decided to dig down to see what lied below. No bodies here. What they found were two baskets of corn, "some yellow, and some red and others mixed with blue." This discovery, combined with the nearby cornfields, inspired them to name the area Corn Hill.

The fields and the buried baskets of corn had not been abandoned, as the Pilgrims wanted to believe, but had only been stored underground to be used the following season by the local Pamet Indians. Knowing they had no way of getting seed for the next year, the Pilgrims justified stealing the corn by saying they were only "borrowing" it and would repay the owner once they found out who it was. Today, a small bronze marker notes the historic spot where the Pilgrims stole as much corn as they could carry back to the *Mayflower*.

After returning to the ship and reporting what they had found, the weather turned frigid and stormy – karma, perhaps? Despite several inches of snow and freezing winds, the Pilgrims continued looting the stockpiled mounds around Corn Hill during the course of the next two weeks. When all was said and done, they had "borrowed" ten bushels of corn.

The Pilgrims considered this cache of corn a blessing from god, and it did help to sustain them through the following year in Plymouth. It was, however, these presumptuous acts of pilfering that made for an interesting 'first encounter' with the Indians on December 8, 1620, as told in the next story.

EXPERIENCE

Follow in the colonial footsteps of adventurers past. Take Route 6 to Truro and head down Castle Road to the expansive, peaceful Corn Hill Beach. Paved roads and plentiful parking makes your trek to Truro's only public bay side beach much easier than that of the pilgrims. Clean portable restrooms make it more comfortable too. Take a break from the beach with an easy, shaded 1/3-mile hike along Pilgrim's Spring Trail in North Truro. This requires backtracking north toward Provincetown on Route 6, then making a right at the Pilgrims Heights sign. The trailhead begins near the shelter at the end of Pilgrim Heights Road. This short loop trail provides lovely vistas over the Atlantic, sand dunes and Pilgrim Lake. Keep your eyes open for a marker commemorating the Pilgrims original explorations.

Find a map of this and other trails online at the Cape Cod National Seashore. Website: *www.nps.gov/caco*.

6

FIRST ENCOUNTERS

EASTHAM
– 1620 –

For nearly a month, the Pilgrims had been searching Cape Cod in vain for a suitable place to build their new colony. In early December of 1620, seventeen "discoverers" took the shallop out for what would be their third and final expedition. This group included Captain Myles Standish, John Carver, William Bradford, Edward Winslow, Edward Doten, John Tilley, Edward Tilley, John Howland, Richard Warren, Stephen Hopkins, John Allerton, and Thomas English – many names we grew up familiar with from history class. Five sailors from the *Mayflower* crew, including master gunner Robert Coppin, were also part of this excursion.

The group set sail south along the west coast, intending to "circulate that deep bay of Cape Cod." The weather was so cold that the spraying seawater froze to their clothes, making them feel "as if they had been glazed" according to one man. They continued looking for fresh water and rivers or bays near high ground that might be deep enough to dock the *Mayflower*. They made very slow headway being assaulted by the brutal December elements and frigid winds.

The ship sailed beyond what is present–day Wellfleet and by nightfall it approached the area that is now Eastham. Edward Doten noted ten or twelve Indians busy doing something on the beach, but the natives ran off into the woods when they saw the explorers coming.

The discoverers brought their battered little boat ashore. Night was falling when they set up camp to spend the night on the beach. They constructed a primitive barricade of logs and thick pine boughs by the light of a much needed fire. The shelter was as tall as a man and open on one side, protecting them from the wind, the cold, and a possible attack.

Billowing smoke from another campfire meant that a group of Natives were about 5 miles away. It was safe to assume that if the Pilgrims could see the Indians' fire, then the Indians could certainly see theirs. Guards were put in place and the men tried to get some sleep.

The next day was spent exploring the area in two groups; one went by water and the other by land. The first group took the shallop and sailed along the coast, anxious to find a substantial river. The second group trekked through the hills, following Indian tracks past a graveyard, abandoned Indian summer houses, and cornfields. They eventually came upon the Indians' campsite from the night before, discovering the remains of a large black fish like a grampus, or dolphin. But overall they deemed the area uninhabitable and kept moving. Once again, the Pilgrims' search for a permanent dwelling site proved futile. There were no rivers or suitable land. Cape Cod really was just a marshy, sandy bay.

As the sun set, the two groups met back at the shallop. They had supper and made their barricade as they had done the night before. Around midnight, they heard a "hideous and great cry," after which the guardsman called "Arm! Arm!" The men jerked from their sleep and grabbed their muskets. After shooting off a few rounds into the air, the noise stopped. One of the seamen convinced the others that he heard these same screeching noises from wolves, or similar wild beasts, while in Newfoundland. The group attempted to go back to sleep, but the remainder of the night must have been a restless one.

In the wee hours of the morning on Friday, December 8, 1620, the Pilgrims said their prayers, had breakfast, and began carrying their things down to the boat to move on. All of a sudden, the same "great and strange cry" that had woken them only five hours earlier once again filled the air. One of the men in the company began shouting "Indians! Indians!"

Unfortunately, most of the guns had already been packed into the boat, and as they scurried off to recover their arms from the shallop, the Indians sent arrows sailing into the camp and began to descend upon the barricade. At this point, only four men in the camp had loaded guns. It was five o'clock in the morning and the sun had not come up yet, so two of the men shot into the darkness, while the others stood ready to fire as soon as they had a visible shot. Once the other pilgrims retrieved their guns from the boat, they began to fire into the woods, scaring the Indians off as quickly as they had come. Surprisingly, no one was killed or injured on either side despite this quick and violent exchange of fire.

Arrows had pierced the barricade and made holes in the men's clothing hanging on its walls, but since not one of the men was hurt in this conflict, the Pilgrims believed they were protected by God's divine providence. As proof, they sent a bundle of Indian arrows back to England, telling tales of their vanquished enemies.

A plaque located at Eastham's Town Hall commemorates this skirmish between the Pilgrims and Indians. As already mentioned, this was by no means the first meeting between Europeans and the Native Americans of Cape Cod, but the Pilgrims' first hostile encounter with the locals left such an impression that they decided to name the location First Encounter Beach, which it remains to this day.

EXPERIENCE

The only skirmish that happens here today is an occasional battle for prime position to watch the sun set. First Encounter Beach is arguably the best place on Cape Cod to watch the sun sink into its final blaze of glory—although, any west facing beach can claim the same beautiful sunset. Eastham's west facing bay side beach is situated on a small peninsula where the Herring River meets the bay. It is a bit off the beaten track and requires some navigating from Route 6, but this beach is worth seeking out—especially if you want to impress your sweetheart with a romantic sunset walk. The expansive flats are fun to explore by day too. It is also a mellow place to let the kids play and explore tidal pools as the water trickles in and out.

Remember that even though First Encounter seems like a cozy neighborhood beach, there is the usual charge for parking from May through September. Be aware that with warm summer evenings come biting flies and throngs of sunset gawkers parked in cars or sitting in camp chairs with camera in hand. However, in off–season you could quite possibly have the beach to yourself and free parking. Whether visiting by day or night, it is difficult to escape the thought of what a special place this is—from both a historic and scenic perspective.

7

BOURNE FREE ENTERPRISE

BOURNE
– 1627 –

The sixteenth century British colonists helped to shape various political, social, and religious foundations of the United States. We learn in elementary school that the Pilgrims signed the Mayflower Compact, which loosely sets the tone for the democratic groundwork of our country. But, a more obscure piece of pilgrim history that rarely turns up in the classroom, is the establishment by the English colonists of the Aptucxet Trading Post. It is the first recorded commercial trading site in America—a venture that most historians consider to be an economic cornerstone of the our country.

In the winter of 1622, the Pilgrims had been in the New World for only two years. The novice pioneers were in dire need of supplementary food having not yet mastered the New England climate and soil. As a result, their crops did not produce enough to support the colony through the winter.

In utter desperation, a reconnaissance mission was launched in search of food. After trekking 20 miles south of Plymouth they happened upon a Wampanoag village along the shores of the Manomet River, just at the edge of the Cape. In an act not unfamiliar to our modern American behavior, they purchased so much corn they were unable to carry it all back to Plymouth in one trip. A local native named Cawnacome stored the excess corn until they could return for it, which would prove to be a turning point in the Pilgrims' plight for financial security.

After depositing the first supply of corn back at the plantation, a smaller group returned to retrieve the rest. Upon their arrival, they learned that Cawnacome was fishing three miles farther down river at Aptucxet, a name which means, "little trap in the river." When the Pilgrims went looking for Cawnacome, they discovered the area in which they would establish their first moneymaking enterprise five years later.

It is important to know that before coming to the New World in 1620, the Pilgrims signed an agreement with the London Company, which funded their passage to America and the ongoing settlement of the new colony. The contract with the English investors originally stated that the settlers would own their homes, their livestock, and would work for the company five days a week with two days to work for themselves. This seemed an acceptable arrangement, but a game changer was about to happen.

The plans were in place for the *Saints and Strangers* to set sail for America on the *Mayflower*, but shortly before leaving, the terms of the contract were drastically changed to the extreme benefit of the London Company. The revised agreement stated that the colonists owned nothing until all debt was repaid. The travelers, if they still wanted to go, had little choice but to sign on for seven years of servitude to the London Company.

During the first few years, the London Company continued to subsidize additional settlers from whom they required repayment, therefore, adding to the debt of the original colonists. If that wasn't bad enough, the investors raised the interest rates several times on the amount that was owed. The Pilgrims' debt was growing as fast as the they could make payments. Finding a way to pay this off as quickly as possible was of great importance in order to realize their original dream.

The light bulb moment came in 1627 when the Plymouth "think tank", comprised of a few enterprising business minds, recalled the winter they had gone in search of Cawnacome and ended up at Aptucxet. During that journey, they learned that the Manomet and Scusset Rivers provided easy east to west access between Cape Cod Bay and Buzzards Bay. However, between the two rivers, there was a one half mile stretch of land over which the boats had to be carried. A shortcut across the shoulder of the Cape would allow flat–bottomed boats to navigate the rivers rather than sailing the whole way around the peninsula.

This safe inland location, and the shorter route to the regions south of Cape Cod spawned an idea to establish a small trading post. Aptucxet's fresh water source made it a desirable site, enabling the trading post to be staffed year round. Them to choose this site, as it enabled it trading post to be staffed year–round, leaving someone to guard the goods. England readily gave permission to set up shop.

A wood–framed building of hewn oak planks was built using a construction style typical of the seventeenth century. The structure was anchored into the ground with posts and wooden latticework filled in with a mixture of mud, clay, animal dung, and straw to create the walls (called wattle and daub). This one–room shop might have been whitewashed to protect it from the elements, but it might also have been sided with clapboard, like the homes of Plymouth Plantation. One thing is for certain about the trading post—its roof was made of wood boards which were not thatched, as were many of the early colonial homes. At the time Aptucxet was built, straw roofs were considered a fire hazard and deemed illegal.

This enterprising group of men began trading up and down every river, bay, and inlet south to the Connecticut River. They traded with the Dutch in New Amsterdam (present–day New York) and with the local Natives. Within a short time, the entrepreneurs began shipping furs to England by the boatload. The booming trade business quickly necessitated the use of a currency system, so Aptucxet instituted the wampum (a cylindrical, polished fragment of a clam's shell)—making this the first commercial enterprise in the New World to use local currency on a regular basis.

The Pilgrims may have conceived, set up, and run the business, but at the end of the working day, the profits from the Aptucxet trading post belonged to the London Company. The successful business allowed them to eventually pay off the entire colony's debt.

This small business venture set the stage for important events that occurred the following year. According to Governor William Bradford of Plymouth, the Aptucxet Trading Post financially saved the colony. Prior to 1627, most of the North America's settlement were crown sponsored. Kings and Queens footed the bill for overseas exploration and settlement. In return, they were entitled to the riches of the New World. By the 1620s, private investment companies in England and Holland financed many of the new colonies. In this case, the private investors rather than the monarchy were paid the profits—such was the situation at Plymouth. Repayment terms were about to change.

In 1627, the Pilgrims' contract with the London Company expired without having been paid off, so eight residents of Plymouth drew up a contract of their own to privately expedite the repayment of debt. William Bradford, William Brewster, Myles Standish, Edward Winslow, John Howland, Thomas Prence, John Alden, and Isaac Allerton proposed that they (along with four others from London) would pay the debt for all 250 people in the colony if they could have ownership of Aptucxet. This included exclusive rights to trade in the area, two boats, and everything in stock. In other words, they wanted a monopoly.

The London Company wanted their money back and agreed to the new terms, signing the contract in the fall of 1627. The Pilgrims' negotiation for the Aptucxet Trading Post became America's first private business contract, which established the country's first private business.

The site of the original Aptucxet Trading Post is located just over the canal on the Cape side, in present–day Bourne. The original building was destroyed in a hurricane in 1635, but rebuilt. The fresh–water spring that kept the business afloat is still visible today. Though few detailed records exist of this little trading post, there is no denying the important role it played in the development of free enterprise in America.

EXPERIENCE

Learn more about America's first privately owned business by visiting the Aptucxet Trading Post Museum (24 Aptucxet Road / *www.bournehistoricalsociety.org*), located off Shore Road along the Cape Cod Canal in Bourne Village. Just look for the windmill–turned–art gallery at its entrance. The existing museum, although a replica, is built on top of the trading post's original foundations. It also incorporates some original elements from the 1627 structure, making this a special building within the realm of rare Colonial period architecture. This important place is often overlooked given its close proximity to other popular early American historical sites, like Plymouth and Boston. But, it is exactly this convenient location that made Aptucxet such a success. Not only can you see archaeological finds from the original site, but you'll learn about Pilgrim and Native American lifestyles, wampum currency, the types of goods traded, and colonial food and medicinal traditions in the wildflower and herb gardens. A visit to Aptucxet takes about an hour, making this a great picnic stop when cycling along the canal, as well as a fine educational experience for family members of all ages.

Make a day of it by visiting a few other interesting historical sites around Bourne. Lovers of presidential history should head over to the Gray Gables Railroad Station, named for President Grover Cleveland's summer home on Monument Neck in Bourne. The depot was built as a private train stop at his sprawling estate, Cape Cod's first Summer White House. Unfortunately, the house has since burned down, but the train station was moved to the Aptucxet property in 1976.

The Aptucxet Trading Post Museum Complex is operated by the Bourne Historical Society at the Jonathan Bourne Historical Center (30 Keene Street, Bourne). It is open seasonally, from Memorial Day to Columbus Day.

8

THE LANDS OF NAWSETT

EASTHAM

– 1646 –

Eastham, one of the Cape's four original towns, may not be its oldest, but it is the only one founded entirely by the same settlers of Plymouth Colony. In 1620, when the Pilgrims first arrived in the New World, Myles Standish and his expedition had a conflict with the local Nauset Indians at present–day Eastham. The group was so affected by this experience that they named the site First Encounter Beach then promptly abandoned the area for fear of a second encounter. More than twenty years would pass before the Pilgrims made their way back to Cape Cod from the mainland.

During the 1630s, Plymouth was a fully functioning colony and the Pilgrims' debts to the London Company investors were paid off. Many of the residents had become dissatisfied the poor soil, the small land grants, and the overcrowded village. At one time or another, many of the original settlers contemplated returning to Cape Cod, but two decades passed before this came to fruition.

In 1640, Governor William Bradford defined the Cape in a patent to the Earl of Warwick in England. He described "that tract of land lying between sea and sea," using its Indian name of Nawsett, which means "at the river's bend." The boundaries included most of the present–day Lower and Outer Cape: Brewster, Harwich, Eastham, Wellfleet, Provincetown, Truro, Orleans, and parts of Chatham. The lands of Nawsett were reserved, by British government decree, for "Purchasers" and the "Old Comers" — those families who paid the colonists' way out of debt, and those who came to the New World aboard the first three ships: *Mayflower, Fortune,* and *Anne.*

In 1643, an expedition was sent to Nawsett to determine the potential of moving the entire Plymouth colony back to the place where they had first arrived in the New World. After a few scouting missions and despite finding harbors and an abundance of shellfish, the area was deemed incapable of sustaining such a large number of people. Instead of bypassing the opportunity altogether, the colony purchased tracts of land from local Indians. In April of 1644, the colonial court of Plymouth gave permission for seven families (forty–nine people in all) to "go to dwell at Nauset."

This group included both Old Comers and Purchasers. Edward Bangs, Eastham's first treasurer, was considered both. He was born in England and arrived in Plymouth Colony in 1623 aboard the *Anne*. He became a great landowner and was licensed to sell wine and strong waters in Nauset, "provided it be for the refreshment of the English and not the Indians." He lived in Eastham until the ripe age of eighty–seven.

Josias Cook, the town's first constable, and Richard Higgins, a highway surveyor, were from two of the seven original families to settle in Plymouth, and both made the move to Eastham, where like Edward Bangs, died well into old age. It must have been the fresh Atlantic air. Deacon John Doane however, outlived them all. He was 110 years old when he died in 1707, and according to tradition, was rocked in a cradle during several of his final years.

Nicholas Snow, a true "gentleman of Eastham" and the town's first clerk, came to the New World aboard the *Anne* and was married to Constance Hopkins, who arrived aboard the *Mayflower*. Her fellow passengers, Giles Hopkins (no relation) and Lieutenant Joseph Rogers were also among the first families to settle in Eastham. Both men are buried alongside Constance in Eastham Cove Burying Ground, which is located near the site of the town's original settlement.

It was under the leadership of Thomas Prence that Eastham grew and its agricultural and fishing economy prospered. The fertile, sandy soil was perfect for growing asparagus and turnips. So much so, that Eastham was considered the asparagus capital of the (known) world well into the twentieth century.

Thomas Prence was born in England and arrived at Plymouth Plantation aboard the *Fortune* in 1621, shortly after the first Thanksgiving was held. He made his money as one of the eight members of the trade monopoly of Aptucxet, but was best known for his leadership roles within Plymouth Colony. Following the death of William Bradford in 1657, Prence was elected governor of the colony, but chose to live in Eastham.

Prence and his wife, Patience Brewster (daughter of Elder William Brewster), were residing in Duxbury when seven families, including his own, decided to establish a new town out on the Cape. His farm, which included the town of Eastham, was said to have been the "richest land in the place." Prence's property holdings were extensive even by today's standards, as he owned the land around modern–day Harwich, Brewster, Wellfleet, and Truro. As Henry David Thoreau walked the cape he wrote in his book *"Cape Cod"* about the legendary pear tree brought from England by Prence which stood near the farmhouse until it was blown over in 1849. The pear tree may not exist today, but the original stone doorstep from Prence's Eastham home is located at the base of Pilgrim's Monument in Provincetown.

Prence might have been considered a just and qualified leader of the town, but his puritanical tendencies surfaced in the form of intolerance and open criticism of most other religions. When Quaker missionaries arrived on Cape Cod from England in the 1650s, they received the same sort of rejection that had driven the Puritans from their motherland to the New World. Prence enforced the imprisonment and punishment of anyone who supported the Quakers. In an ironic twist of fate, his daughter eventually married a Quaker and provided him with several Quaker grandchildren.

Once settled, Nauset was designated an official township within two years. It was incorporated on June 2, 1646, and was officially named Eastham in 1651. But as early as 1654, the large township was being partitioned off. A few Old Comers had claims to the western half of Eastham, which soon became Harwich, while William Nickerson claimed what would eventually incorporate as Chatham.

By the mid 1700s, towns like Wellfleet and Orleans had also broken off from Eastham, causing what was originally the Cape's largest town to become one of its smallest. Eastham held the hearts of many of the Pilgrims who returned there to live out the rest of their days. The surnames of America's earliest settlers continue to permeate the town's census list and its cemeteries. In Eastham's and other Cape Cod burial grounds, some of the America's earliest sculptural carvings exist on some of its oldest tombstones. Tomb hunters are never disappointed as Cape Cod cemeteries contain a veritable who's who among pilgrim settlers; many for whom streets and landmarks are named and whose ancestors still reside on the Cape.

EXPERIENCE

Eastham, the Gateway to Cape Cod's National Seashore has attracted generations of visitors and, like the founding families, they return year after year. To experience a little piece of pilgrim history, visit the Windmill on Village Green, just off of Route 6. As the oldest windmill on Cape Cod, it stands as a symbol of Eastham's colonial heritage even though it was moved around a few times before permanently landing here.

Eastham resident, Thomas Paine built the mill in Plymouth around 1680 and ninety years later, it was shipped across Cape Cod Bay on a log ferry to Truro where it began life anew on the Cape. By 1793, the mill was situated near Salt Pond in Eastham then relocated one last time to its current location on the site of an earlier mill, also owned by Paine. During the summer, sneak a peek at the internal workings of Eastham Windmill on tours conducted by the Eastham Historical Society (*www.easthamhistoricalsociety.org*). The windmill also serves as the backdrop for concerts, art festivals, and other celebrations, including the annual Windmill Weekend held each September. A visit to Eastham Mill is educational and fun at the same time.

Eastham's Historical Society also operates a number of lovely historical sites worth a look, including the c. 1869 Schoolhouse Museum on Nauset Road, near the Cape Cod National Seashore Visitor Center. Exhibitions highlight the town's history, from Native American artifacts and shipwrecks to a children's one–room schoolhouse, where kids are encouraged to have a hands–on experience in a schoolroom setting from bygone times.

Another Eastham landmark showcasing life from colonial through Victorian period is the Swift–Daley House on Route 6, near the Eastham Post Office. Unique architectural features, period furnishings, and decorative arts in this c. 1741 home offer a glimpse into pre–Revolutionary Cape Cod. The historic home takes half of its name from Nathanial Swift, one of the principals of the Swift Meat Packing Company (founded in 1855 and now owned by JBS, one of the world's largest meat processors) who lived here in 1859. The second half of the name is derived from Mr. and Mrs. Raymond Daley, who purchased the house and funded its restoration.

Whether you travel to Eastham for its centuries of history, the beautiful Atlantic and bay side beaches, or kayaking or hiking in the Great Marsh, the Eastham area holds ceaseless appeal for those who return each season. The town's original settlers would be proud to have set this precedent.

9

LEGEND OF
THE WHYDAH

WELLFLEET
– 1717 –

C aptain "Black Sam" Bellamy wasn't always a pirate. He was born around 1690 in Plymouth, England—a known breeding ground for some of history's most notorious buccaneers. When one grows up dirt poor, living in the dodgy shadows of the docks, whispers of remarkable wealth and worldly adventures seems an enticing career choice. Bellamy watched and learned as great seafaring bandits such as the grandfather of piracy, Henry Avery, and the crown–sponsored privateers, John Hawkins and Francis Drake, came and went from Plymouth port.

Unhappy with his life in the bottom tiers of English society, Bellamy made his way to the New World for a new beginning. The penniless man arrived in Cape Cod in 1714, at the age of twenty–four. Shortly after, he met and fell in love with a Wellfleet girl named Maria Hallett. While on the Cape, Bellamy clocked a lot of hours at the Great Island Tavern—a smuggler's den full of black–market goods and rowdy sailors. Luckily, this clandestine pub operated by island–owner Samuel Smith, was situated on a small island two miles from the town of Wellfleet—far from prying eyes. It is here Bellamy heard tales of Spanish treasure sunken off the coast of Florida and decided there were riches to be had at sea.

With little convincing, a local jeweler named Paulsgrave Williams financed Bellamy's venture. They bought a sloop and gathered a crew, but unfortunately, by the time the *Marianne* reached Florida, the gold had already been recovered by a number of people, including the Spaniards, English privateers, and other pirates of the Caribbean.

Disappointed, but not discouraged, Bellamy rallied his men to become official looters of nations, free men—Pirates! They hoisted the Jolly Roger, a black flag emblazoned with skull and crossbones, and "Black Sam" was on his way to becoming one of America's most feared and revered pirates.

Bellamy learned the art of high–sea crime from pirate–turned–pirate–hunter Benjamin Hornigold and spent time carousing with another soon–to–be–infamous student, Edward "Blackbeard" Teach. Together, they terrorized the West Indies and by early 1717, Bellamy was the scourge of the Caribbean. With more than 200 men under his command, he seized booty from more than fifty ships. At the peak of his terror, Black Sam possessed five ships, including the *Whydah*—his prize, which he personally captained.

Bellamy had spent several days chasing the *Whydah* around the Caribbean, before finally capturing the ship of every pirate's dream: a galley with a huge cargo space full of gold and silver, and loaded with armament. With enough treasure to last a lifetime, Black Sam and his crew decided it was time to retire. The plan was to sail north to Maine after retrieving Maria from Wellfleet, then live off their spoils. No one anticipated the tragedy that would soon befall them all.

As the pack of pirates sailed from the Caribbean along the Atlantic coast of America to Cape Cod, they plundered every ship they encountered. By the early morning of April 26, 1717, the *Whydah* was bursting at the seams with booty: ivory elephant tusks, sweet molasses, and heady rum, not to mention countless precious coins and gold bars. "Could it get any better?" Black Sam thought to himself. Of course it could!

As they approached Nantucket, the crew seized a merchant ship from Dublin, which was carrying 7,000 gallons of Madeira wine. Much to the dismay of the *Mary Anne*'s captain, Bellamy's men boarded the ship and forced it to join the *Whydah* on a northwesterly course—but only after indulging in the captain's private stash of booze! The wine was a fine prize, but Bellamy was thinking more of Maria when he steered the ships toward Wellfleet, a fatal move that marked the beginning of the end of the *Whydah*.

As the laden ship lumbered along what is present-day Chatham, thick fog was setting in. Knowing the waters were shallow and the shoals dangerous in this part of the Cape, Bellamy bided his time and waited for a break in the weather. When a small sloop named the *Fisher* slowed down near the *Whydah*, its captain had the misfortune of admitting to knowing the waters. Being late in the afternoon, Bellamy sent a few men aboard to seize the *Fisher* to help navigate the *Whydah* and *Mary Anne* through the potentially treacherous waters.

Slowly, they made their way up the east coast of the Cape with *Mary Anne* leading the way. The wine–filled, hundred–ton galley was followed by the *Whydah,* with the *Fisher* bringing up the rear. As it grew darker, the fog grew thicker and the waves began rising. The *Mary Anne* started to lag behind, but the *Whydah* persisted. Being mid–April, Black Sam assumed storm season was over so he forced the ships to press on, not realizing a powerful arctic wind blowing down from Canada was about to hit them head on.

By nightfall, the *Whydah* was out of sight of the *Mary Anne* and the *Fisher,* both of which had run aground. Their crews were arrested the next morning and jailed in Eastham. The *Whydah* had to keep going north, since this particular type of ship, a galley, could not handle high winds. Sailing due north, however, was impossible. The seventy–mile–per–hour winds drove the ship west toward land, into the dangerous breakers.

Over and over, the words "Breakers! Breakers!" were screamed above the howling rain. Bellamy ordered the men to turn the boat around and drop the main anchor, hoping they could ride out the storm without hitting land. The crew made several valiant attempts to turn the ship into the waves to avoid being capsized. It worked a few times, but inevitably, the strength of Mother Nature was just too much for the 146 mortals aboard the *Whydah.* The ship ran aground only 500 feet from shore and a little before midnight on April 26, 1717, the ship rolled, sealing the fate of all aboard, including that of Black Sam Bellamy.

Waves began heaving over the boat, dumping tons of water onto the deck and sweeping many of the men out to sea. The main mast broke off and floated away. Water quickly filled the cargo area below. Anyone lucky enough to escape being drowned below deck would not have lasted more than a few minutes in the frigid water, and then any survivors would have had to struggle 500 feet to shore and up the steep, sandy hillside.

As the *Whydah* flipped over, all the valuables in the cargo space crashed about the ship. Many of the crewmen were crushed. Even worse than death by gold bullion, is being pinned to the bottom of the ocean by cannons or other heavy, quick–sinking objects. The pirate's spoils became their headstones. In the blink of an eye, 144 lives were lost.

The next morning, more than a hundred bodies washed ashore—mutilated, swollen, and unrecognizable. It is rumored only two men survived. Did the Pirate Prince go down with his ship or was Black Sam one of the survivors? No one knows for sure. As for the pirates sent from the *Whydah* to seize the *Mary Anne* and the *Fisher*, their fate was no better than those aboard the doomed ship. On October 22, 1717, the group was tried in the Boston Courthouse and eventually hung for piracy.

The treasure of the *Whydah* remained a legend for more than 250 years. It took Barry Clifford, a dreamer who grew up on Cape Cod, to continue the *Whydah's* story, which is told later in "Ghost Ship Rising."

EXPERIENCE

This experience introduces one of Cape Cod's hidden natural gems, but requires a bit of planning and preparation. Dig out your sturdy boots to hike the seven–mile trail around Great Island, which today, is actually a peninsula protecting Wellfleet Harbor. Three centuries ago, this small finger of land was a legitimate island, but over the centuries sandbars grew and marshes filled in what was once a watery moat, dividing the Great Island from Wellfleet center.

According to legend, this playful poem welcomed thirsty patrons to the now non–existent Tavern on Great Island:

Samuel Smith, he has good flip,
Good toddy if you please,
The wav is near, and very clear,
'Tis just beyond the trees.

Begin your trek from the parking lot where there are picnic tables and portable restrooms. The marked trailhead leads out past the protected strip of sand known as "the Gut" and "beyond the trees, " to where the poem once lured Black Sam out onto the Great Island. The beach and wooded trails surrounding the Gut are fairly rugged. This particular stretch is one of Cape Cod's longest, continuous expanses of undeveloped beach. Embark on this experience expecting less than pristine moments, biting flies, and the occasional dead bird. The trade–off? Respite from the overcrowded oceanfront beaches, great outdoor exercise, and on a clear day, sweeping views into Provincetown.

A few words of care: it might be tough, but try not to step on fiddler crabs as this protected area teems with shellfish and the sea birds who feast upon them. Never give in to the temptation to loot exposed oyster beds. Wellfleet's clam cops take this very seriously and will seize your booty and impart a hefty fine.

The remoteness and serenity of Great Island will certainly make you feel like Robinson Crusoe, if not a pirate. The seven–mile round trip trail leads through dunes and forest, and past the site of Great Island Tavern and a Wampanoag monument. Plan to bring your own food and drink, as all that remains of Samuel Smith's swashbuck-ling pub is a plaque and splendid views of Wellfleet Harbor. Despite beautiful water everywhere, there is not a drinkable drop of water along this trail.

Travel as light as you can, especially when hiking to the southern most point known as Jeremy's Flats. During low tide, one is able to walk all the way out to Jeremy's Point. Save room for bug spray, particularly in summer months. This is not an option, as gnats, flies, and tics are equally drawn to Great Island. But most importantly, pay attention to the tidal charts. Even though the water rolls in and out twice a day in a timely manner, a little "creative hiking" might be required if the tide unexpectedly catches up with you during your return trip. With proper planning (and lots of insect repellent), this is one of the most magical—and potentially thrilling—hikes on the Cape. Take the trail less traveled.

10

THE FIGHT FOR FALMOUTH

FALMOUTH
– 1779 –

The jagged jetty of land protruding southwest from the Cape is not unlike the craggy Cornwall coast stretching southwest of England. Here, explorer Bartholomew Gosnold's home port of Falmouth was the namesake for this Cape Cod village, which was incorporated in 1686. Its busy harbor served as the stage for British raids during the years leading up to the Revolutionary War. A few years later, it was one of the few Cape towns fired upon by the British.

Cape Cod was drawn into the colonies' plight for independence when Britain banned the use of Boston Harbor. Local Tea Act protesters boarded a British ship and dumped its contents overboard. After the infamous Boston Tea Party in 1774, residents of Cape Cod to helped to sustain the city of Boston during this blockade with provisional contributions.

The American Revolution began the following year, in 1775, when British troops were sent to destroy the weapon depots in Concord, Massachusetts. Along the way, 700 militiamen warded off more than 1,700 of England's finest—and the war had begun. By January 1776, George Washington was raising an army of which 260 men came from Barnstable County in which Falmouth is located.

Because of its expansive coastline, Cape Cod became a major player in the role of our young country's defense. One of the largest regiments was made of soldiers from Falmouth, Sandwich, Barnstable and Yarmouth. A seasoned veteran of the French and Indian War, Joseph Dimmick of Falmouth, was appointed the Lieutenant Colonel to oversee this huge contingent. Dimmick was given sufficient forces to patrol the islands around Cape Cod and the authority to arrest anyone who might be supplying the enemy with provisions.

A few months later, when the Battle of Bunker Hill was fought in Boston, the tide of war drifted to the doorstep of Cape Cod. When the Declaration of Independence was signed on July 4, 1776, the Cape's residents pledged undying support. Battle followed battle, and British ships gathered in the waters of Buzzard's Bay, making it obvious that the coastline south of Boston Harbor had to be heavily protected.

Sixty whaleboats were purchased and delivered to Falmouth Harbor where the militia was training to defend this strategic position on the southern side of the Cape. For a year, the British captured ships in and around Falmouth, ransacking and confiscating their supplies, but come September 1778, Colonel Dimmick had had enough.

While training the Falmouth militia on the village green, Dimmick rallied his men and took three whaleboats out against the British navy, which resulted in regaining a schooner that had been seized earlier. Many historians consider this to be the first naval victory in American history, but it would be a few years before the British Royal Navy would admit they had underestimated the vigor and vigilance of the Continental Navy. While Joseph Dimmick was a key player in this triumph, he is best remembered for the events on April 3, 1779.

On April 2, 1779, Dimmick received word of an imminent attack on Falmouth. He was warned that the British were coming to burn the town and capture Woods Hole. With the Cape Cod militia on full alert, more than 200 men made their way to Falmouth in less than a day. They dug out trenches along the shore of what is now Surf Drive, settled in and waited through the night for the British to arrive.

As the early morning fog lifted off the waters of Falmouth, the militiamen saw ten British vessels anchored and ready to lay waste to the town. The ships bombarded Falmouth for five and a half hours with the intention of coming ashore to loot the town of its supplies and weaponry. But Dimmick and his volunteer militia never budged. The British attempted several times to make landfall, but were repelled by return fire of 200 brave Falmouth patriots. King George's ships eventually pulled out and vented their frustration on Nantucket Island. This was not exactly a pivotal moment in the Revolutionary War, but it showed the colonists' clear resolve to win their freedom. It is this sort of sacrifice that helped to secure the future of a new country.

EXPERIENCE

From Falmouth, take a short drive along Surf Drive (a.k.a. Beach Road) en route to Nobska Lighthouse. You'll pass by Salt and Oyster Ponds, the area where the colonial militiamen hunkered down for the night. Nobska Point marks the division between Buzzard's Bay and Vineyard Sound. The beacon was originally built in 1828 and is now listed on the National Register of Historic Places. Catch the magnificent views over the sound as ferries shuttle travelers to the Vineyard from nearby Falmouth Harbor.

Continue from Nobska Point following Church Street as it turns into Woods Hole Road and runs along Falmouth's harbors. Eventually, you will come upon Woods Hole Oceanographic Institution (WHOI)—the country's largest ocean research center. The museum's interactive exhibition space showcase a gamut of watery objects ranging from shipwreck artifacts to high—tech equipment used in deep ocean discoveries. If visiting during the summer, plan in advance to take the guided tour of the facility during which you are given a wonderful history of the institute and can take a peek into 'restricted' areas.

Just around the corner from WHOI is Woods Hole Science Aquarium, the nation's oldest public marine center, established in 1875. The small aquarium houses about 140 species of marine life common to New England waters, which can be explored through touch tanks, behind—the—scenes tours, and an outdoor seal habitat reserved for those unable to be released into the wild. Try to visit around opening or later afternoon to see the seals being fed. Admission is free.

Visit Falmouth's Town Hall to see contemporary murals depicting the history of the village, including *The Battle of Falmouth* by artist, Karen Rinaldo. This image appears at the beginning of this chapter..

11

JEREMIAH'S GUTTER: CAPE COD'S FIRST CANAL

ORLEANS
– 1804 –

Everyone knows that you aren't officially on Cape Cod until you cross the bridge over the world famous canal, but what many people might not know is that this isn't the first man–made waterway cut across the peninsula. More than 200 years before the opening of the Cape Cod Canal, many of the region's earliest explorers, including Bartholomew Gosnold and the Pilgrims, recognized the need for a direct passage between Cape Cod Bay and the bodies of water surrounding the Cape. Early settlers had the vision, but not the technology to make it happen. For another century, sailors and explorers continued to navigate from the bay into the Atlantic along the treacherous shoals around the outer Cape.

During seasonal high tides, salt water floods into the marshy regions around present–day Orleans. For hundreds of years, streams trickled eastward from Cape Cod Bay converging daily with the waters of the Atlantic in Nauset Harbor. As the bodies of water mingled together, they created a shallow, natural waterway on which small boats could pass between the bay and the ocean. This now–forgotten passage ran through the property of Jeremiah Smith along the border of what is now Orleans and Eastham. Historians call it "Jeremiah's Drain," but locals used a more colorful term, referring to the watery old ditch as "Jeremiah's Gutter."

As Cape Cod's population and commerce grew, so did the need for a shortcut between the bay and the Atlantic. The journey from Provincetown Harbor to the south side of the Cape was lengthy and treacherous, especially around the choppy, shallow shoals of Truro and Chatham. Near the elbow of the Cape, a narrow, low–lying ridge of land separated Cape Cod Bay from the Atlantic Ocean. During high tide the water from the bay would overflow across this swampland, completely isolating the northern part of the Cape. This type of flooding might have given Bartholomew Gosnold the false impression that Cape Cod was an island when he was exploring the area in 1602.

In the spring of 1717, the residents of Eastham decided to deepen this natural, one–and–a–half–mile channel running across Jeremiah Smith's land. They hand–dug the passage, which connected Boat Meadow Creek on the bay side with Town Cove on the Atlantic side, and called it "Jeremiah's Gutter." As the name suggests, this channel was very narrow and more akin to a creek than a canal, but it served its purpose—sometimes. Boat traffic was subject to the whims of Mother Nature. When tides and sandbars cooperated, Jeremiah's Gutter could accommodate boats up to twenty tons. This convenient waterway also slashed shipping time around the Lower Cape by a full day.

Shortly after it was completed, the new "canal" was put to immediate use at the order of England's King George I. His privateers were sent to locate and retrieve the treasure from the wreck of the infamous pirate ship, *Whydah*. Captain Cyprian Southack sailed from Boston through Cape Cod Bay and out to the Atlantic via Jeremiah's Gutter. But despite the new shortcut, Southack was too late to locate the loot. He arrived well after the *Whydah* and its golden contents had settled to the bottom of the ocean—only to be discovered 250 years later.

When Orleans broke away from Eastham in 1797, Jeremiah's Gutter formed the northern boundary of the new town. In 1804, the canal was further widened and improved allowing this humble waterway to play an important role during the War of 1812. Local sailors used whaleboats to transport much-needed supplies and to smuggle salt through the narrow canal when British warships blockaded Cape Cod Bay. Large English warships in the Atlantic Ocean were unable to sail near Orleans because of the shallow shoals, making it impossible for the British to gain control of this small, but vital, passage.

In 1865, Henry David Thoreau briefly mentioned the "canal" in his book titled *Cape Cod*. As Thoreau and a friend trekked on foot through the region, he wrote about the difficulty traveling through the waterlogged lands around Orleans. He also confirmed the importance sailors placed on any sailable passage through the Cape by noting that even the smallest channel was important and usually dignified with a name—even if it was just a ditch full of water.

By the late 1800s, plans for the new Cape Cod Canal were underway and the use of Jeremiah's Gutter declined. A few proposals suggested the gutter be turned into a toll waterway, but those plans never came to fruition. Even if the ditch was larger, the extreme tidal flats of Cape Cod Bay created problems for big ships. Shifting sandbars just off Chatham on the Atlantic side presented problems for everyone. Due to the impractical location, sandbars, and the extreme tides Jeremiah's Gutter eventually fell into disrepair then silted over.

The only evidence that remains of Cape Cod's first 'canal' is in Orleans' namesake streets, Canal Road and Smith Lane, and a historic marker commemorating the point where the two bodies of water most likely met to create the passage. The historic plaque stands in Orleans about a tenth of a mile off of the Eastham/Orleans rotary on Route 6, diagonal from a Wendy's restaurant. The next time you drive through the roundabout or are wandering around the shops near Town Cove remember that you are on the site of Cape Cod's original canal, Jeremiah's Gutter.

EXPERIENCE

One can easily cruise what was once Jeremiah's Gutter via kayak at high tide. Boat Meadow River on the bay side of Eastham is the launching point for a five–mile round trip paddle, which stretches across the elbow of the Cape, almost into Town Cove. The river meanders under a bridge, through marshlands and along Boat Meadow Bog. Be aware that the current is swift during mid tide, so paddling up current results in a rigorous journey through the narrow stretches. The river–turned–creek is navigable as far as the Cape Cod Rail Trail then trickles out only 500 feet from Orleans Rotary. This is the end of the road, so to speak, as no water route exists to cross from here into Town Cove, which is less than a quarter mile away. Perhaps, we should rally to bring back Jeremiah's Gutter and somehow reconnect the two. To access Boat Meadow River, take the Rock Harbor exit at the Orleans Rotary. Make a left and follow Bridge Road out to Bayview Road.

After finishing an oh–so–close crossing of the Cape, complete your journey in Orleans with a different rite of passage—a hot fudge sundae at Sundae School Ice Cream shop (210 Main Street, East Orleans). The family run, old–fashioned ice cream parlor has been slinging scoops for almost forty years from their Dennisport shop. It has been consistently voted best ice cream on the Outer Cape since it opened in 1986. For so many people, summer is not complete with a stop in to one of the Sundae School locations (606 Main Street/ Route 28, Harwich Port and 381 Lower County Road, Dennisport). The shops are open seasonally, but Dennis Public Market (Route 6A, Dennis Village) carries their ice cream quarts year round.

12

AMERICA'S WONDERBERRY

DENNIS
– 1810 –

From the first Thanksgiving table to Ocean Spray's jiggly jelly to a modern day "superfruit", the cranberry has become synonymous with Cape Cod since its first recorded cultivation two hundred years ago. Yet, this wonderberry was in use long before the Europeans took to farming it on a large scale. The native Pequot Indians of Cape Cod took full advantage of the bitter fruit's natural attributes, using it in a versatile range of culinary, medicinal and household products. Nowadays, we take for granted all of the different forms in which we find the cranberry, but the humble fruit still remains one of only three native North American berries that are commercially grown in the United States—the other two being blueberries and Concord grapes. Cranberry bogs are now developed throughout peaty wetlands in many northern states, but commercial cultivation began around 1810 in Dennis.

The English colonists arrived in the fall of 1620 to discover Cape Cod Bay covered in vines bursting with wild, garnet–colored berries, which were dubbed "craneber-ries." At first glance, the pink, flowery blossom resembles the head and beak of a sandhill crane, and looks even more so when bobbing in the wind. Like several other wild, northern red berries, the craneberry was sometimes referred to as "bearberries," because, you guessed it—bears were often spotted eating them.

While the European settlers recognized this shrubby evergreen as a valuable barter-ing item, the Native Americans were the first to actually make extensive domestic use of this versatile berry, which they called sassamanesh. The fruit was used to dye woven material, served as a healing agent for wounds, and most popularly as a dietary staple. The Nauset Indians boiled and mashed the red, waxy berries together with deer meat to make a jerky that could be stored for a very long time. The Native Americans realized its capacity to preserve food, as well as its medicinal and nutritional value, which came in handy for the Pilgrims as they battled disease and starvation in the early years.

Cape Cod's coastal ecosystem has never been conducive to conventional farming, which is why the original colonists chose not to settle here in the first place, but wild cranberries (along with turnips and asparagus) thrive in the Cape's sandy peats. Cranberries require growing conditions unfamiliar to the English settlers who were more accustomed to traditional agriculture. This unusual fruit does best in shallow "bowls" of land filled with sand and water, but do not grow consistently from year to year when left to their own device. By 1800, many locals already laid claim to their own personal cranberry yards, from which they would harvest a supply of berries for the winter. But, the yield varied dramatically depending on environmental factors. It was far from a reliable crop.

In 1810, Revolutionary War veteran, Captain Henry Hall was working on his farm in North Dennis along the bay side of the Cape. While clearing a bit of land near the beach, he came upon a patch of cranberry vines that had been covered by windblown sand. He noticed clearly that the vines seemed to be thriving rather than dying off. It was a 'Eureka!' moment. Captain Hall transplanted several vines into a fenced area, purposefully spreading sand over them. Then he waited and maintained the sand blanket. Come springtime, the vines were flourishing, and by autumn, they produced many more berries that were bigger than ever.

Captain Hall's fortuitous discovery, keen observation, and intuitive experimentation led to him being recognized as the first person to successfully cultivate cranberries. It also paved the way for the local fruit to become a viable commercial crop and profitable source of income. Word of Hall's new "sanding" technique spread quickly, spawning copycat farmers, including his neighbor, Eli Howe who's Howe Cranberries are among the most famous today.

Throughout the early nineteenth century, the number of growers rapidly increased, and by the late 1840s, the commercial center for growing cranberries shifted from Dennis to its equally boggy neighbor, Harwich. The cranberry industry took root in in this region for its ideal soil conditions and extended growing season. This led to further experiments and innovations, paving the way for the large–scale and lucrative cranberry business with which we are familiar.

Captain Alvin Cahoon is another one of the industry's earliest pioneers. In 1846, he planted "eight rods to berries" in the Pleasant Lake district of Harwich, creating the country's first commercial cranberry bog. Innovation must have run in the Cahoon family as the following year, Alvin's cousin, Cyrus also began cultivating cranberries at Pleasant Lake. Cyrus Cahoon revolutionized the industry by building the first level–floored cranberry bog, which 150 years later, is still in production. He also developed the "Early Black" variety of a deep red (almost black) berry that his wife discovered at Black Pond in Harwich. Today, the "Early Black" and "Howe" varieties comprise 95% of the cultivars grown in Massachusetts and are the two most popular cranberries found on our Thanksgiving tables.

Throughout the 1850s and '60s, the cranberry industry flourished due to a combination of successful cultivation techniques and outside economic forces. Still, it wasn't the cash crop the innovators anticipated. For thirty years, cranberry farming remained more of a supplement to Cape Cod's other agricultural crops, asparagus and turnips, and maritime industry…and then it happened! "Cranberry Fever" struck in the middle of the nineteenth century and it couldn't have come at a better time.

The decades after the Civil War were depressing as the bottom fell out of Cape Cod's two major industries—fishing and shipbuilding. Iron steamships replaced the wooden boats built on the Cape, while fish from the West Coast, Great Lakes, and other inland water sources became more accessible because of the expansive new railroad system. The final blow to Cape Cod's economy came during the late 1800s, when the whaling industry all but disappeared because of over–fishing.

A majority of the Cape's unemployed or retired seamen now needed full or supplemental income for their families. Those who owned marshy land looked to the berry for a new livelihood. Luckily for them, as the number of cranberry growers continued to increase, so did consumer demand. Five acres of cranberry bogs provided a reasonably comfortable existence for a farmer, but owning ten boggy acres afforded an entire family the high life. In 1881, the Cape Cod Cranberry Grower's Association was formed and remains one of the oldest farmer organizations in the country.

As the cranberry business evolved, so did new manufacturing processes which allowed white sugar to be available for everyday use. By the early twentieth century, the naturally tart cranberry blended with sweet processed sugar became popular in sauces and everyday recipes. In the 1930's, Ocean Spray was established as a small, grower–owned company just off of Cape Cod near Plymouth, with cranberry sauce and bottled fruit juices among their early products. By the 1960s, the Cape Codder cocktail, a mixture of vodka, cranberry juice and lime, became one of the most popular mixed drinks in America. Today, American farmers harvest approximately 43,000 acres of cranberries each year, with almost half coming from Cape Cod. As the leading agricultural product of Massachusetts, the cranberry remains essential to the economy of Cape Cod.

EXPERIENCE

Cranberries are one of three fruits indigenous to North America, as well as blueberries and Concord grapes. The cranberry harvest runs from mid–September through October. Each autumn the flaming red fruits of Cape Cod's cranberry bogs are celebrated at the Cranberry Arts and Music Festival in Harwich (*www.harwichcranberryfestival.org*). The free two–day event, held shortly after Labor Day, marks the end of summer with a Cran–Jam of local musicians and more than 100 artisans selling crafts, art, and cranberry products. The family–friendly festival is a great way usher in autumn, but if you happen to miss this two–day window, the full cranberry experience is still possible by taking a bog tour.

The Capes 14,000 acres of working cranberry bogs provides a variety of opportunities, ranging from buying fresh cranberries in–season to getting an in–depth look at the harvesting techniques. Weather and season certainly dictates the visitor schedule, but check with the Cranberry Growers Association (*www.cranberries.org*) for a list of farms and what each has to offer by way of products and tours.

The Harwich Historical Society located within the Brooks Museum (80 Parallel Street, Harwich / *www.harwichhistoricalsociety.org*) is a good place to start. The exhibitions display artifacts and historical information related to the cranberry industry along with hands–on, family–friendly activities. After an educational museum visit, hop aboard one of the daily organized Cape Farm and Cranberry Company Bog Tours (1601 Factory Road, Harwich / *www.cranberrybogtours.com*). During the guided tour, learn about the year–round operation of a working cranberry farm and wet picking. Then visit with the farm animals and spend some time shopping for cranberry items in the market. Reservations are highly recommended for this tour.

On weekends during harvest season, schedule a tour to see the dry–picking form of cultivation at Annie's Crannies (*www.anniescrannies.com*). The family–run cranberry farm in historic Dennis Village has long been a part the Cape's cranberry tradition. Its gift shop is open through mid–November and carries fresh fruit and other handmade cranberry products, such as candles, honey, and jam.

Should you visit outside of harvest season, plenty of local shops carry cranberry products all year. Check out the various farmer's markets during the summer, general stores, hotel gift shops, and neighborhood boutiques in most of the Cape Cod's towns.

13

FALMOUTH
UNDER FIRE

FALMOUTH
– 1814 –

In 1803, the American Revolution was barely over and the country was pulling itself up by its bootstraps when Napoleon Bonaparte's aggressive politics pitted England and France against one another. The United States was one of the few countries to preserve its neutrality and remain at peace with the two nations. This created an unprecedented flourishing of commerce, particularly on Cape Cod, due to its seafaring business. This prosperity was not to be enjoyed by the citizens of the United States for long.

Three years later, Napoleon declared all British territory in a state of blockade. Trade and correspondence with Great Britain was prohibited. Consequently, American commerce suffered two blows. First, ships carrying cargo between the United States and England were at risk of seizure by French fleets. Second, the British government toughened their stance, prohibiting even neutral countries to trade with any nation at war with England. Consequently, neutral American vessels trading with France would be confiscated.

In response, the United States government, under President Thomas Jefferson, placed an embargo on all exports to these two countries. The embargo was very unpopular with Americans due to its disastrous affects on their maritime interests. Few suffered more than the people of Cape Cod, who were dependent on trade with Europe and the West Indies for their very existence.

The embargo was repealed by Congress in 1809, only to be followed by another even more restrictive act completely prohibiting all trade with France and England. This strict law, however, was ineffective in forcing the British and French governments to change their position on confiscating American ships, which was becoming fatal to coastal commerce. It was just a matter of time before America declared war against France or England, or both—but what would it be? The persistent interception of American ships by the British made the decision an obvious one. President James Madison declared war against England on June 10, 1812, thus commencing the War of 1812.

The residents of Cape Cod were not eager for this conflict, but they knew it was necessary and unavoidable. Local militias, which had not seen action since the Revolutionary War, were called to defend their towns as best they could. Once the news reached England that war had been declared, British ships began to assemble up and down the New England coast, and its towns were soon under attack. Massachusetts Bay came entirely under control of the British early in the war, thwarting communication between Boston and other commercial ports.

British war ships began cruising every nook and cranny around Cape Cod, raiding harbors and burning boats that attempted to run supplies or trade goods. No part of the state was more harassed than the towns in Barnstable County—Falmouth in particular.

Falmouth's strategic location on the south facing side of the Cape allowed the Falmouth Artillery Company to fire regularly on British ships in Buzzards Bay. In turn, Falmouth was under almost constant attack by the Royal Navy. Some Cape Cod towns, such as Brewster and Eastham, paid a handsome price to British commanders to avoid being bombed or ransacked, but Falmouth refused to sell out.

The *HMS Nimrod*, a British sloop of war, sailed into New England waters in the fall of 1813. This fast, well-built ship was named for an Old Testament hunter, and the symbolism was not lost on the religious folk of Cape Cod. It was part of a squadron sent to seek out, menace and destroy American privateers. The *Nimrod*, under the command of Captain Nathaniel Mitchell, began preying on boats around Cape Cod. By October 1813, it was considered the scourge of Buzzards Bay and Nantucket Sound.

In January 1814, a squadron of British ships, including the *Nimrod*, set up a command post at Tarpaulin Cove in the Elizabeth Islands. They used an inn, well known among local mariners, as their headquarters. On the eve of January 13, 1814, the innkeeper overheard the crew of the *Nimrod* planning an attack on Falmouth. They wanted the city's brass cannons, which were becoming quite a nuisance to the British ships cruising the Cape's southern shoreline. The astute innkeeper had sufficient time to warn the town where the militia was already dug in.

On the morning of January 28, 1814, the *Nimrod* sailed into Falmouth Harbor and dropped anchor. The commander raised a truce flag and sent a small party ashore to demand the town surrender its two cannons and a sloop in the harbor—otherwise, Falmouth would be bombed. This sort of extortion was common all along the coast and the captain had his way with most port towns. But it was not to be the case with Falmouth. Not only was the demand refused, but the commander of the Falmouth Artillery Company, Captain Westin Jenkins, challenged the British by saying, "if ye want the cannon, come and get it!"

Captain Mitchell gave the town until noon to comply, but they had no intention of doing so. There was just enough time to rally the local militia, and remove all the sick, women, children, and prized possessions to a safer place. An hour later, the Battle of Falmouth commenced.

The *Nimrod* spent the better part of the day unloading more than 300 cannonballs on Falmouth. The gunfire finally subsided at night, but the townspeople were uncertain what fate awaited them in the morning. At sunrise, the *Nimrod* unceremoniously pulled up anchor and sailed westward to meet up with another ship-of-war back at Tarpaulin Cove.

Fortunately, no one was killed or injured, but several of Falmouth's buildings sustained considerable damage during the futile shelling of the town. In fact, a few still show the scars of cannonball fire, including the defunct Elm Arch Inn, built in 1810, where a cannonball hole remains in one of the parlors and another in the men's room of the Nimrod Restaurant, where men and women alike have sneaked a peek into the restroom. Sadly, neither of these places are currently open for business. Hopefully, any new owners will preserve these ragged spots where cannonballs were lobbed as a tangible bit of military history.

On June 13, 1814, the *Nimrod* ingloriously ran aground after successfully attacking and burning seventeen ships in Buzzards Bay. It is believed the crew frantically dumped several of its cannons overboard, to lighten the load in order to sail away. In 1987, divers recovered five cannons from the waters of Buzzards Bay. One of these cannons can be seen at the Falmouth Historical Society, which proudly proclaims "the British never got our cannons, but we got one of theirs."

EXPERIENCE

We are not going to pretend that this stand-off was a pivotal event in the War of 1812, but it certainly attests to the resolute nature of the Falmouth residents to stand their ground and resist bullying from the enemy. The earlier story *Fight For Falmouth* reinforces this point.

Today, it might be difficult to get up close and personal with some of the spots where the infamous cannonballs were lobbed, but the Falmouth Historical Society and Museums on the Green (65 Palmer Avenue / *www.museumsonthegreen.org*) contain a treasure trove of artifacts and information about the history of the town, including the shelling by the *Nimrod*. The museum campus, located at 55 and 65 Palmer Avenue, is centered on Town Green where the colonial militia once practiced.

Exhibits are held in both the Cultural Center and the c.1730 Conant House, where the Historical Society offices are located. Expert guided walking tours leave from here each Tuesday and Thursday morning at 10 a.m. Purchase tickets from the Museum Center, located in the rustic Hallett Barn.

Admission includes a visit to the c.1790 Wicks House, where visitors get an intimate look into the life of the eighteenth century doctor, Francis Wicks. Beautifully manicured grounds around the museum complex include a Colonial Garden, Herb Garden and Memorial Park maintained by the Falmouth Garden Club. As a whole, the collections of period furniture, textiles, paintings, and historical documents speak to the rich history of Falmouth, while changing exhibitions highlight different aspects of the town's role in Cape Cod history. Its famous sons and daughters are also represented here. One of the more famous being Katharine Lee Bates, author of the song, *America the Beautiful*. She was born in Falmouth in 1859 and penned the words to her iconic anthem in the summer of 1893.

America the Beautiful

O beautiful for spacious skies,
For amber waves of grain,
For purple mountain majesties
Above the fruited plain!
America! America!
God shed His grace on thee
And crown thy good with brotherhood
From sea to shining sea!

O beautiful for pilgrim feet,
Whose stern, impassioned stress
A thoroughfare for freedom beat
Across the wilderness!
America! America!
God mend thine every flaw,
Confirm thy soul in self-control,
Thy liberty in law!
O beautiful for heroes proved
In liberating strife,

Who more than self their country loved,

And mercy more than life!

America! America!

May God thy gold refine,

Till all success be nobleness,

And every gain divine!

O beautiful for patriot dream

That sees beyond the years

Thine alabaster cities gleam

Undimmed by human tears!

America! America!

God shed His grace on thee

And crown thy good with brotherhood

From sea to shining sea!

Katharine Lee Bates

14

KEEPING THE BRITISH AT BAY

ROCK HARBOR
– 1814 –

Cape Cod was particularly vulnerable during the War of 1812 and served as a backdrop in a great number of naval conflicts. Rock Harbor, located on the west side of Orleans, is a relatively narrow and shallow inlet that serves as the town's gateway into Cape Cod Bay. This tranquil cove was the site of a skirmish between locals and the British navy on December 19, 1814.

In direct response to Britain's imperialistic whims, the United States declared war on Great Britain on June 10, 1812. The British monarchy sought to block and seize American vessels and prevent foreigners from emigrating in an effort to limit the young country's growth and prosperity. Residents of Cape Cod, knowing well the negative effects war would have on the maritime industry, were not particularly supportive. Despite the American government's embargoes against England, much illicit business was carried on between American traders and British officers. Eventually, the United States government was driven to enforce laws prohibiting all trade with Britain.

When the war began, the British government initially enforced a state of blockade around the Delaware and Chesapeake regions only. There was a certain amount of mutual need between the United States and Great Britain. England very much needed American supplies to provision its army in Spain, while the Cape Codders wanted to maintain their livelihoods. For a brief time, both sides remained willing to do business with one another in some capacity. As the war developed, the blockade was extended along the south coast, and by May 1814, to the whole east coast, including Cape Cod.

In 1813, a few individuals from the town of Orleans laid out a road leading to Rock Harbor where they built a protected landing place for boats. These individuals originally claimed the land as their personal property, but written deeds or titles could not be produced. Rock Harbor was legally deemed to be town property. Orleans agreed to pay the for the training of a militia to protect the area, which was heavily patrolled by British ships.

By 1814, the size and strength of England's Royal Navy allowed it to blockade all of the ports around Cape Cod Bay, from Provincetown Harbor to Falmouth.

American ships that were caught running supplies or trading goods were seized and its crew members were taken prisoner. The British war ships raided the Cape's harbors, sometimes indiscriminately, and burned boats at will. Threats of bombardment and destruction caused the people of Cape Cod to become vigilant of the British vessels hovering around their shores.

Orleans appointed a Committee of Safety and guards were placed on the west shore to sound an alarm if the enemy should attempt to carry out their constant threats. As an added safety measure, the townspeople formed a secondary artillery regiment should their formal militia be called to duty in another town leaving them unprotected. A representative was sent to Boston to request the government supply them with proper weapons, but he was refused and returned to Orleans without munitions. British landing parties began making good on their threats. They ravaged the countryside, stealing crops and livestock, and threatened to destroy the valuable salt works and other properties in the towns. Some of the less scrupulous British commanders demanded payment from the townspeople in exchange for not attacking them. Captain Richard Ragget of the *HMS Spenser* was among those who demanded ransoms, earning his nickname, the "Terror of the Bay."

Another ship, the *HMS Newcastle*, which was part of a squadron led by Commodore George Collier, captured American privateers and harassed the cape's coastal towns. The British demanded that the town of Orleans ante up a hefty sum of $1,000 for the safety of its citizens; otherwise the town would be bombed and the local salt-works destroyed. The neighboring towns of Eastham and Brewster had already paid handsomely to save their saltworks, but Orleans refused the insulting proposition.

Fortunately for Orleans, the heavily armed ship–of–war was too large to enter the harbor and navigate the marshy Rock Harbor Creek. Several barges full of British soldiers were sent ashore, but the harbor's watchful guards had sufficient time to alert the militia. Men quickly arrived from Orleans and the neighboring towns. After a short skirmish, the militia drove the enemy back to their ship, with only one British casualty.

After the failed landing attempt, the *Newcastle* began firing its cannons but was too far offshore. The cannonballs fell short. Unable to get any closer to Rock Harbor Creek, the battle ship gave up and went in chase of the *U.S.S. Constitution*, famously known as "Old Ironsides." Five days later, on Christmas Eve, 1814, the Treaty of Ghent was signed and the War of 1812 came to an anticlimactic close. The large and intimidating *Newcastle* lived out a mundane career until it was eventually disassembled and sold for scrap in 1850, while the *Spenser* met a similar end in Plymouth, England in 1822. The *U.S.S. Constitution*, built in 1794, outlived them all and remains the world's oldest commissioned naval vessel still afloat.

Orleans led a peaceful existence until another attack occurred a century later during World War I. This time, the action took place on the Atlantic side of the town as relayed in the upcoming story, *Assault on American Waters*. No physical evidence exists of the Rock Harbor battle, yet one can easily imagine the intimidating war ships hovering along the coastline while the earliest American patriots stood their ground. Nowadays, tranquil Rock Harbor is known best for its chartered fishing excursions and fiery sunsets.

EXPERIENCE

When driving along Route 6 through Orleans, history buffs will appreciate a quick detour into quaint Rock Harbor, home to New England's largest charter fishing fleet. May through October, Rock Harbor Charter Service (*www.rockharborcharters.com*) offers anglers a chance to reel in everything from bass to sharks during half and full day fishing excursions on one of their fishing boats. As a tidal harbor, the departure times correlate with the tide, so check the online schedule and to make reservations.

Landlubbers can stay near shore and keep their toes in the sand or venture out onto the one of the country's largest tidal flats. At low tide, it is easy to walk a mile out into Cape Cod Bay, exploring the sandy flats dotted with marsh grass and rippling tidal pools—an exciting prospect to see what lurks beneath the bay as its underwater environment becomes exposed during low tide. But trek cautiously and be aware of the tidal schedule as the incoming water often creates tidal creeks between sand bars. Whether on foot or boat, either adventure brings a perspective to how far out the British ships were anchored as they attempted to bring Rock Harbor into submission.

After working up an appetite from fishing or exploring, head for the little, shingled house near the entrance to the harbor. Young's Fish Market (113 Rock Harbor Road / *www.nausetfish.com*) is a superb choice for anyone in search of a delicious and reasonably priced lobster roll. A few doors down at 117 Rock Harbor Road is yet another purveyor of fine, fresh fare. If you are in the mood for fish and chips or fried clams, look no further than Cap't Cass. Not much has changed since opening in the 1950s, including the simple décor and lack of air conditioning. In fact, Young's and the Cap't are two quintessential, unadulterated clam shacks that travelers seek out for an authentic Cape Cod eating experience. Cash is king at both establishments, so make sure you have money on hand as neither accept credit cards.

Grab some grub, settle in somewhere on the rocks, and soak in the atmosphere. It does not get any more experiential than eating the catch–of–the–day while watching the tide roll in to picturesque Rock Harbor along with the fishermen and their haul. Time your visit for the late afternoon and stick around for sunset. Being on the west side of the Cape, beach goers are treated to some of the most extraordinary sunsets right up until the moment the sun dips below the horizon.

15

A SAILOR AND
AN EMPEROR

BREWSTER
– 1815 –

Historians are full of "what ifs." What if, after the battle of Waterloo, Napoleon Bonaparte escaped to America rather than surrendered to the English? What if he had taken up residence on Cape Cod—or in New Jersey, where his brother, Joseph Bonaparte had emigrated? Though it is just a matter of speculation today, Captain Jeremiah Mayo could have changed the course of history by carrying out plans to smuggle Napoleon to America in 1815. Granted, most of this story is hearsay, but use your imagination…

Mayo was born in Brewster on January 29, 1786. He was the son of a blacksmith, but developed a taste for life at sea after spending the summer following his fourteenth birthday fishing the Straights of Bell Isle in Newfoundland. By the age of eighteen, he convinced his reluctant father to allow him sail to the Bahamas for a valuable load of salt. How does a father argue with a son who is articulate, headstrong, and 6 feet, 4 inches tall? He doesn't.

This marked the beginning of what would be many trips for Jeremiah to the Caribbean and Europe, particularly to French ports of call. Mayo made his first voyage to the southern French city of Marseilles in 1804—the same month Napoleon Bonaparte proclaimed himself emperor and sold the Louisiana Territory to American.

During the next few years, while sailing around the Mediterranean, Captain Mayo visited many places associated in one way or another with the Bonapartes. His ships carried cargoes of fish, flour, cider, and wine to and from the ports of Malaga, San Sebastian, and Gibraltar in Spain; Lisbon, Portugal, and even as far north as Amsterdam.

The southwest coast of France was a region Mayo frequented, sailing into Bordeaux to replenish his stash of high–end wines. During an 1808 visit to another coastal city, Bayonne, he encountered the legendary Napoleon on horseback rallying his army to invade Spain.

Mayo's ship was under constant threat of seizure and came under attack by British warships while in the Atlantic and Mediterranean. His admiration of Napoleon's military prowess is understandable. But Captain Mayo's high regard for the Emperor was not necessarily the consensus. Thomas Jefferson, for instance, believed Napoleon to be a tyrannical monster that was undeservedly admired. Still, the post–Revolutionary War sentiment was such that many Americans felt continuing contempt for the British, often embracing the enemies of England as friends of the United States—including Napoleon, tyrant or not. The British hitting too close to home may have been another reason Capt. Mayo appreciated Napoleon's efforts.

In the early months of 1809, Mayo made his way back to his farm in Brewster, where he married Sally Crosby. He spent the next two years sticking close to the Cape and was one of ten delegates selected to represent his hometown at meetings about another potential war with Great Britain. Once the War of 1812 broke out, Mayo was back to running cargo across the Atlantic.

Jeremiah Mayo made several trips to Sweden, Germany, Belgium, and even England in his swanky new ship, the *Sally,* named for his new bride. He managed to out-maneuver British sloops with his fast brig and regularly carried European goods back to Boston and Cape Cod. Mayo was especially renown for his uncanny navigational skills and keen judgment. As Captain, he never lost a man nor suffered a wreck – not even when New England's harbors were chock–full of enemy warships. His reputation preceded him everywhere he went, including France.

While America was standing its ground during the war with Great Britain, Napoleon was losing his. On April 12, 1814, the Emperor unconditionally abdicated the throne and was sent into exile on the island of Elba, just off the coast of Italy. In less than ten months, Napoleon had plotted his escape and by March 1815 he was back in France marching to Paris. For 100 days, Napoleon was once again the ruler of France, but the rest of Europe was not going to let it be without a fight.

Napoleon led his troops into Belgium in June, where they battered the Prussian army. However, the British troops at Waterloo proved to be too much. On June 18, 1815, British and Prussian soldiers under the command of the Duke of Wellington defeated Napoleon's forces once and for all at the famous Battle of Waterloo.

In the weeks following Napoleon's second abdication he returned to Paris to plot his next strategy. The idea of seeking refuge in the United States came up in conversation with one of his closest aides. Coincidentally, Captain Mayo was in France a few weeks after the battle. He docked the *Sally* in the port at Le Havre on France's northwest coast, conveniently close to Paris. Was Mayo here for more wine? Was he aware that an agent of Napoleon Bonaparte would interview him?

Knowing Mayo's reputation for avoiding the British fleet, one of the Emperor's aides sought out the captain to inquire if he might be able to smuggle "precious cargo" into the United States. There was an unspoken understanding of what a dangerous undertaking this would be. If the ship was captured or searched, it would result in the confiscation of the vessel and more importantly, the detainment of all aboard. It is quite possible Mayo consented.

A French paper dated June 30, 1815, claims that Napoleon left Paris with six carriages en route to the west coast of France. According to the article, he was attempting to flee the country. It also stated that a large American ship was awaiting his arrival. Could it have been the *Sally*? That same month, the emperor's brother wrote a letter to their sister stating that, "Napoleon will depart for the United States… where all of us will join him."

The British caught wind of Napoleon's plan and sent ships to blockade ports up and down the northern coast of France. They searched many of the ships that were leaving the harbor before allowing them to sail away. A popular story claims that Napoleon held Emmanuel Courvoisier's cognac in such high esteem that his get–away ship was stocked full of barrels. When the ship was searched, British officers sampled the brandy and were so impressed they nicknamed it Le Cognac de Napoleon for the Emperor. The term Napoleon Cognac stuck. Neither the cognac nor the Emperor ever made it to the United States.

On July 17, 1815, Napoleon had the misfortune of being intercepted in Rochefort, France by the British, very close to where the American ship was supposedly waiting for him. Rather than flee, Napoleon surrendered—he would not abandon the soldiers who supported him. Once Captain Mayo learned that Napoleon had surrendered to the British, he hastily returned to Cape Cod. It is presumed that had Napoleon made it to the boat, he would most likely would have safely escaped to America as Jeremiah Mayo sailed the *Sally* from France to Boston without encountering the British.

Napoleon was not given asylum in England as expected but was quickly deported to the prison island of St. Helena, where he lived the remainder of his life in exile. Though the disgraced emperor did not end up in America for his "retirement," some of the Bonaparte family did. His elder brother Joseph settled in Bordentown, New Jersey, and bought land in upstate New York. Lake Bonaparte is a reminder of what could have been. Napoleon realized the mistake he had made in a letter written to his sister, expressing his regret over not making it to America. In January 1816, he began taking English lessons, supposedly to be able to read what the English newspapers were saying about him, but who knows? Perhaps Napoleon had another great escape up his sleeve.

Captain Mayo resigned from sea life in 1819 to lead the Brewster Artillery Company, and then became the president of the Brewster Marine Insurance Company. In 1881, a friend wrote, "General Mayo was a man who had seen a great deal of the world and had rare conversational powers to tell stories that created pictures of places and scenes." One is left to wonder how Jeremiah Mayo told the story of plotting Napoleon's escape to America and whether he too speculated, "what if?"

EXPERIENCE

Even though Napoleon did not make it to America, there is plenty of French culture represented on Cape Cod. Casual cafés and fine dining bistros offer a gamut of prix fixe menus, escargot, pâté, éclairs, and of course, Courvoisier.

For a wide range of pastries, coffee, and brasserie style meals check out the bakery–bistros at Pan d'Avignnon (15 Hinckley Road, Hyannis / *www.paindavignon.com*) and PB Boulangerie (15 Lecount Hollow Road, Wellfleet / *www.pbboulangeriebistro.com*). Both turn out exceptional breads, tarts, and bakery lunches of things like quiche and croque sandwiches.

For a slightly higher end Francophile dining experience, Bleu (10 Market Street, Mashpee Commons, Mashpee / *www.bleurestaurant.com*) serves lunch, dinner and a jazzy Sunday brunch, while L'Allouette (787 Route 28, Harwich Port / *www.frenchbistrocapecod.com*) is open for dinner. Each offers multi–course fixed price menus and a fine wine and spirits list. Visit the bar at the Captain Linnell House (137 Skaket Beach Road, Orleans / *www.linnell.com*) for a bowl of bouillabaisse or a Cognac night capper. The trés romantique dining room at this historic 1840's inn is a beautiful setting for a date night dinner complete with lobster bisque and Crème Brulée

You will shiver with *oh la la's* knowing classic French fare is never too far away!

16

SANDWICH GLASS:
ON THE CUTTING EDGE

SANDWICH

– 1825 –

SANDWICH GLASS: ON THE CUTTING EDGE

In the middle of the nineteenth century, when many of Cape Cod's towns were prospering from maritime industry and beach resorts, the village of Sandwich was garnering international acclaim as a center for world–class glass–making. In 1825, a distinguished and colorful entrepreneur, Deming Jarves left Boston's New England Glass Company to establish his own Sandwich Glass Manufactory on Cape Cod.

When the time came to set up shop, a few bay side locations were on Jarves' radar. Having previously hunted in the Sandwich marshes, he knew this terrain would be able to provide the massive amount of timber required to fuel the furnaces. Jarves also knew Sandwich's shallow harbor would come in handy for shipment of the products. Whispers of a canal connecting Cape Cod Bay and Buzzards Bay made this location even more desirable as it was situated very close to what might be the entrance to the canal so Cape Cod's oldest town would soon play host to one of the most cutting edge businesses in the country. The following year, his business was incorporated as the Boston and Sandwich Glass Company. It was met with instant success, but few envisioned just how definitively this company would revolutionize the glass–making industry.

Jarves was an experienced china merchant and well educated in glass technology and trends. It is not an understatement to say he was very much ahead of his time. This visionary man built employee housing around the factory, aptly dubbed Jarvesville, then hired a logging company to clear 2,000 acres of forest for its wood, forever altering the landscape of the Upper Cape. Frustrated with the railroad system and its steep shipping fees, he circumvented the need for trains by commissioning a company steamship to be built. Most importantly, Jarves brought some of the world's most skilled glassblowers from England, Ireland, and New England to this tiny village. In less than a quarter century, Sandwich was the most prosperous town on the Cape.

At its peak, the company employed upward of 500 people. Highly skilled craftsmen made exquisite objects d'art that bring big bucks at today's auctions. These artisans put Sandwich Glass on the map. The less skilled glassworkers turned out an endless number of practical mold–blown pieces like candlesticks, decanters, and glasses—items that were affordable for the average wage earner.

The Sandwich Glass Company came in to its own at the peak of the Industrial Revolution. It was the first factory in the country to adopt the process of semi–automation to make glassware—yet another testimony to Jarves' vision. While Jarves may not have invented the lever–operated glass–pressing machine, he patented ways to improve upon it and implemented large–scale production for the first time. Machinery combined with the introduction of coal furnaces, which could now be heated 300 degrees higher—allowed for larger, more elaborate patterned glassware to be made. Between the 1830s and 1850s, the automatic process rapidly evolved. Surface imperfections on the earlier machine–made "Lacy" glass quickly gave way to a stunning spectrum of colorful, perfectly pressed molded tableware.

The Sandwich Glass Company was the first to manufacture full sets of glass tableware. Despite mass–production, it maintained a reputation for creating high quality pieces—particularly, lighting devices—a difficult standard to sustain in the machine era. Yet, this process marked a definitive end to the handcrafted way glass has been made for thousands of years. With half a ton of products being shipped from Cape Cod every week, Sandwich Glass became one of America's largest and best–known glass companies.

In its early years, Sandwich Glass blowers employed the most common and least complicated method of glass–making, but hand–blowing every individual piece was a laborious and costly process. Whale oil lamps were among the earliest free–blown pieces made by these talented artisans. Lamps capable of burning whale oil are an American innovation, but oil–burning lamps, in general, have been in use as far back as prehistoric times, when shells and hollowed–out stones served as reservoirs to hold animal fat and nut oils. The Greeks replaced handheld torches with terracotta oil–burning lamps, while the Romans and early medieval artisans elevated domestic lighting devices to an art form. Advancements in lighting began in earnest during the late eighteenth century, born out of the need for brighter lighthouse lamps. From that point on, developments happened so quickly that new inventions were often obsolete before they even had a chance to catch on.

In 1782, Swiss scientist Aimé Argand designed a smokeless oil–burning lamp that provided seven times the light of one candle—a technology the American government quickly seized upon for its lighthouses. When it came to the average consumer, most liquid fuels were expensive, messy, and often dangerous. Well into the mid–1800s, most households continued to use candles and fireplaces for light, despite smoky candles dripping wax and the offensive odor of burning animal fat or tallow. Oil–burning lamps were rare and expensive in early America, but Sandwich Glass and Cape Cod played their parts in the important, albeit short, history of these specialized lamps.

Cape Cod's whaling industry was, coincidentally, experiencing its heyday when the Sandwich Glass Company was formed. Fishermen discovered that the oil from the heads of sperm whales burned clearer and brighter than most others —and like beeswax, it did not emit a foul odor. The sperm whale, one of the world's largest mammals suddenly became the prime target of New England's already lucrative whale fishery business. Soon, overfishing drove the cost of whale oil beyond the reach of all, but the wealthiest people.

Most families could not afford whale oil, but for those who could, they wanted first–rate lamps to burn their high–quality fuel—yet, no efficient burning systems existed. Whale oil thickens as it cools, so an old burner style was redesigned with a lower wick and flame to keep the oil warm and fluid.

Pairs of whale oil lamps were among the earliest items made when the Sandwich Glass factory first opened. The production life of these lamps mirrored the whale–hunting industry. They were most popular between the 1840s and 1860s, and when the bottom fell out of whaling, the lamps all but disappeared. Sandwich whale oil lamps are now highly collectible and are considered to be among the most beautiful American lamps in existence.

The Sandwich Glass Company is, however, best known for its candlesticks. Even with the coming and going of oil–burning devices, the onset of kerosene burners, and the invention of electric light, candles became less relevant, yet remained an important secondary source of lighting. Not surprisingly, given Cape Cod's watery connection, the most popular Sandwich Glass motif was the dolphin candlestick. The candlesticks featured a dolphin's oversized head resting on the base, while its tail flipped in the air to support the socket for a candle. This design came in a variety of sizes and colors. Dolphin candlesticks were turned out in great quantities for about twenty years between 1850 and 1870, which were copied by factories from Pittsburgh to Czechoslovakia, attesting to the dolphin's trendiness and appeal.

Toward the end of the nineteenth century, trouble was brewing. Competition sprung up throughout the Mid–western coal cities as glassmakers began mass–producing all sorts of affordable tableware, many of which mimicked Sandwich Glass patterns and borrowed the company's pioneering techniques. In the 1880s, when the Boston and Sandwich Glass Company was at its creative and technical peak, problems with the growing labor movement, national strikes, post–Civil War depression, and cheaper Midwestern glass options brought the company to a screeching halt.

On New Year's Day in 1888, the glass factory that lit the way for the entire industry snuffed out its furnaces forever. This fast and furious fizzle out of Sandwich's blazing beacon of success gouged a gaping hole in the town's economy. 75 years would pass before the village of Sandwich would recover from the abrupt closing of one of America's largest glass factories. Eventually, automobiles and new roads brought vacationers and their money; the canal brought shipping and commerce; and twentieth century tourism brought a new appreciation for the Cape—each helping to breath new life into Cape Cod's oldest town.

EXPERIENCE

Experience a bit of the American Industrial Revolution with a visit to the Sandwich Glass Museum (129 Main Street, in downtown Sandwich off Route 6A *www.sandwichglassmuseum.org*), which preserves more than 5,000 pieces of rare glass, including many of the whale oil lamps and candlesticks that lit the way for modern glassworks. The Sandwich Historical Society established the museum in the early 1920s on a picturesque corner in the heart of Sandwich's old village. The beautifully organized collections showcase the company's history and its contribution to the industry on Cape Cod and beyond. Today, one piece of antique Sandwich glass could sell for tens of thousands of dollars, but you can pick up a one–of–a–kind souvenir from the museum gift shop for much less. Commemorate your trip with a paper-weight, jewelry, tableware, Christmas ornaments, or of course, a dolphin candlestick.

The history of Sandwich is brought to life during a Sandwich Glass Museum village walking tour. Docents lead guided, historical tours around the architecture and landmarks of Cape Cod's oldest town, which celebrated its 375th anniversary in 2014. If you prefer a more casual exploration, take a spin through the museum then pop in to Dexter Grist Mill across the street for a tour of a one of America's oldest waterwheel sites. Be sure to pick up a sack of milled corn meal to take home. Also, bring along an empty water bottle to fill from the natural spring that spouts from the fountain near the gristmill. Spend some time wandering the charming side streets of what was once Jarvesville, taking in the Greek–Revival style homes along Jarves, Summer, Liberty and Pleasant Streets, most of which were built between the 1820s and 1860s. Fortify for the next leg of your journey with a bite to eat at the Dan'l Webster Inn—a 300–year–old inn full of antiques and loaded with character (149 Main Street / *www.danlwebsterinn.com*).

Head a mile or so across Route 6A, also known as Old King's Highway, toward Cape Cod Bay. Stroll across the Sandwich Marsh Boardwalk, over the great salt marsh out to the dune–lined beach. This walk sheds light on Deming Jarves' decision to build the factory conveniently near Sandwich Harbor, as well as his decision to use marsh grass as packing material. The landscape, teeming with birds and other wildlife, is beautiful and constantly changing as tidal currents stream through the marsh. What isn't obvious? The now–flat topography was heavily modified, dug out by the company in order to facilitate passage of products from the factory, through the marsh, and out to the harbor for shipping. The boardwalk terminates at Cape Cod Bay. Cross over the protected dunes to Town Neck Beach where boats can be seen entering the Cape Cod Canal. This experience ends fittingly on the site from which countless pieces of Sandwich Glass sailed to homes around the world, putting Sandwich on the industrial map and affordable glassware on the tables of the masses.

17

NANTUCKET BURNING: THE GREAT FIRE OF 1846

NANTUCKET

– 1846 –

etween the years of 1750 to 1850, Nantucket was home base for more than 150 whaling ships, which formed the epicenter of a lucrative deep–sea fishing industry. As the "Whaling Capital of the World," Nantucket Town grew to become Massachusetts' third largest city behind only Boston and Salem. It also ranked among the wealthiest communities in America as vast fortunes were made from hunting humpback, right, and sperm whales throughout the Atlantic Ocean. The refined, clean–burning oil derived from the boiled whale blubber brought immeasurable wealth to the small island.

On the night of July 13, 1846, the worst fire in Nantucket history struck. In the course of just seven dark hours, a centuries–old industry was brought to a screeching halt as a raging fire, fueled by the same oil that brought riches, swept through Nantucket Town, leveling everything. By morning, nearly forty acres lay in ashes, including the commercial district, factories, wharves, and most homes—leaving 800 people homeless. Even the cherished Athenaeum Library went up in flames, taking much of Nantucket's written history with it. This devastating tragedy, now known as the "Great Fire", not only destroyed the entire infrastructure of the city, but also led to the demise of Nantucket's preeminent role in the whaling industry.

Prior to the Great Fire, Nantucket Town experienced a number of blazes, including two devastating fires very close together—one in 1836 and another in 1838. As a result, the Nantucket Fire Department was formed. Fire safety was a primary concern, but little could be done as fireproofing technology did not yet exist. Most of the buildings in the business district were constructed of timber and barrels of combustible whale oil were stockpiled in warehouses along the wharves. This deadly combination of wood and fuel made the downtown area a veritable fire hazard.

Even at the zenith of prosperity, only two brick buildings stood in Nantucket Town: the Old Town Building on Union Street and Rotch Market on Main Street. Everything in between was timber–framed, including most residential properties. However, as ship captains and whaling merchants gained unprecedented wealth in the decade leading up to the Great Fire, this "new money" and social status was touted in the form of opulent brick mansions.

In 1829, the prosperous shipbuilder Jared Coffin commissioned Nantucket's very first brick residence at 19 Pleasant Street, known as Moors End. Elegant brick homes sprung up quickly throughout the neighborhood as members of clan Coffin built mansions at 75 and 78 Main Street. This spawned a competitive streak among local industry barons who were not to be outdone in their living arrangements. Whale oil mogul, Joseph Starbuck built three identical Federal–Greek Revival style houses for his sons a few doors down. In 1845, Joseph Coffin's large, stylish residence on New Dollar Lane prompted Jared Coffin to build an even more extravagant home (presently the Coffin House Inn), at 29 Broad Street.

Unbeknownst to them, this competitive display of wealth along the edge of town would help curtail the Great Fire that roared through Nantucket just a year after Coffin built his second home. Not only would these stalwart structures withstand the flames, their brick walls, slate roofs, and cobblestone pavements would naturally stop the catastrophic blaze from spreading any farther than it did.

Around 11:00 p.m. on the evening on July 13, 1846, a stovepipe caught fire in a downtown hat store. Within an hour the blaze was out of control. Frantic cries of "Fire! Fire!" echoed through town. Nantucketers poured onto the streets to help fight the fiery inferno that was spreading rapidly from one wooden building to another. The fledgling fire department finally arrived with their hand–pumped hose carts, while people scrambled to save whatever they could from their homes and businesses. The streets were cluttered with clothes, furniture, and children covered protectively in wet blankets, but little more could be done.

The harbor was equally doomed. Dozens of whale–oil processing factories and storehouses were clustered along the waterfront. The moment the scorching heat reached the barrels, burning oil spilled across the water creating a sea of fire. All anyone could do was to stand by and watch the island's wealth go up in flames. Locals worked particularly hard to save the Nantucket Athenaeum Library. The building was historically important for hosting a number of the country's most acclaimed speakers, including the likes of Ralph Waldo Emerson, Henry David Thoreau, John James Audubon, and of particular historical importance, Frederick Douglass, who gave his first major speech here in front of a multiracial crowd in 1841. It also housed collections of important documents and artifacts related to Nantucket's maritime industries, as well as fascinating objects brought by whalers from their journeys around the world. Valiant attempts were made to save books, paintings, and sculptures, but to no avail. The fire was just too powerful, and sadly, very little was salvaged.

By early morning, the Great Fire had consumed everything from Rotch Market to the Pacific National Bank on Main Street. The blaze was stopped at Pearl Street (modern–day India Street), but not before destroying more than 250 buildings— including all of the town's markets, shops, seven whale oil factories, twelve warehouses, and three of the four wharfs. One third of the community was burnt to the ground. In terms of today's dollars, an estimated $24 million in damage was done.

Island officials recognized the dire need for help and made a heartfelt plea for aid, which resulted in donations of money, food, and clothing pouring in for those left homeless and jobless. Within a few weeks, reconstruction efforts were underway. It took the tenacious Nantucketers only a few months to rebuild the business district.

With an added emphasis on fire prevention, most of the new commercial buildings and shops were constructed entirely of brick. Additional fire–prevention measures were employed as several hose–cart houses were built in strategic locations for convenient storage of fire–fighting apparatus. One of these small firehouses, known as the Fire Hose Cart House, located at 8 Gardner Street, currently exhibits rare fire–fighting equipment and information about the Great Fire.

In less than two years, a new fireproofed city rose up from the ashes, but the whaling business did not have such a fortunate recovery. The Great Fire destroyed the infrastructure essential to the island's commerce: warehouses, ropewalks, wharves, oil–processing and candle–making factories. The fire was only one of several factors contributing to the downfall of Nantucket's primary industry. Shifting sandbars and the silting up of harbors made it difficult for the increasingly large whaling ships to dock in Nantucket. During the California Gold Rush, many seafarers jumped ship for opportunities on terra firma, seeking wealth in the foothills of the Sierra Nevada rather than on the waves of the Atlantic. A final blow to the whaling industry came in 1859 with the discovery of petroleum, a cheaper form of fuel. Nantucket's glory days were over by the onset of the Civil War.

EXPERIENCE

Dig out your Nantucket reds and hop a boat to "The Faraway Land" 30 miles off the south coast of Cape Cod. It is easy get to Nantucket from Hyannisport on traditional or high–speed passenger ferries operated by Hy–Line Cruises (*www.hylinecruises.com*) and Steamship Authority (*www.steamshipauthority.com*) or from Harwich Port aboard Freedom Cruise Lines (*www.nantucketislandferry.com*). A one–way trip on the slower boat takes about two hours, while the high–speed ferry is well worth the additional fare as it arrives in just under an hour. This is the way to go if you plan to return the same day. So, pack up a beach bag, grab some food and drink from the ferry snack bar and enjoy the ride.

Photo opportunities begin at first sight of land. The iconic lighthouse at Brant Point is the tenth consecutive station to stand watch over Nantucket's picturesque harbor since its establishment in 1746. Gray shingled shacks–turn–shops line the busy wharf. White church steeples peek over trees and rooftops. A constant buzz of people scampering between galleries, stores, restaurants, and boats make for a lively (albeit touristy) vibe all along the waterfront.

Take a little time to wander the cobbled streets through the downtown historic district. It does not take much time to get oriented. For one of the best views looking back over Nantucket Harbor, climb 94 steps to the to the top of the First Congregational Church tower (62 Centre Street / www.nantucketfcc.org). Visit their Website for opening hours.

Today, step back in time to Nantucket's Golden Age. The Whaling Museum (13 Broad Street / www.nha.org), housed in a candle factory built immediately after The Great Fire, tells a compelling story of the boom and bust of the whaling industry. Its permanent collection showcases an impressive 46–foot skeleton of a sperm whale, an 1849 Fresnel lens, lighthouse baskets, captain's portraits, paintings, ivory carvings known as scrimshaw, and souvenirs from around the globe. Enjoy another perspective of the harbor from its rooftop observation deck and see a restored section of the spermaceti candle factory.

Also worth a look is the Egan Maritime Institute – a small, but nicely organized shipwreck and lifesaving museum (138 Polpis Road / www.nantucketshipwreck.org). The private collection consists of maritime artifacts, life–saving equipment, boats, paintings, and objects related to shipwrecks and rescues. The museum is open from Memorial Day through Columbus Day.

There is no shortage of history on tiny Nantucket Island. Its Historical Association, housed in the Whaling Museum, offers the gamut of architectural and historical walking tours, hand–on craft classes, and year–round educational programming. The NHA manages most of the island's major historic properties, so visit their Website (www.nha.org) for hours and admission. The excellent rebuilding and preservation efforts allow more than 800 pre–Civil War houses to remain standing on Nantucket. The island now has more preserved buildings on the National Registry of Historic Places than anywhere else in Massachusetts—including Boston, Plymouth, and Salem.

Two of the not–to–miss historical sites are within easy walking distance of downtown, just on the outskirts far enough to have been spared from the Great Fire. The Jethro Coffin House (6 Sunset Hill Lane), built in 1686, with its restored kitchen and herb garden, is the oldest residence on the island. "The Oldest House" is the sole architectural survivor from the original seventeenth century settlement. It is open for tours from May through October. The Old Mill (50 Prospect Street), built in 1746 by a seaman who had spent time in Holland, is the United States' oldest functioning windmill. The smock style mill is designed so that the top level of the mill can be manually rotated so that the arms face into the wind. Frankly, it takes more time to walk out to the windmill than to actually tour it, but it is worth the three-quarter mile trek.

If walking isn't your thing, consider renting a bike from Young's (6 Broad Street/ *www.youngsbicycleshop.com*) or Cook's (6 South Beach Street / *www.cookscycleshop.com*) bicycle shops or bring your own on the ferry. It is quite easy to peddle around the fourteen-mile long, three mile wide island. The Nantucket Regional Transit Authority (*www.nrtawave.com*) provides a fixed route bus service around the island, providing a quick and affordable way to pop out to the unadulterated beaches of Sconset, Madascet or Surfside for part of the day.

Beer lovers should make the concerted effort to get to Cisco Brewers (5 Bartlett Farm Road / *www.ciscobrewers.com*) for their popular Whale's Tale Pale Ale and Grey Lady Ale. Be sure to eat beforehand or bring your own nosh. This is a drinkin' place and no substantial food is sold on site, although food carts do roll in during the summer. The brewery–distillery–winery is located more than two miles inland, so take advantage of their free courtesy van departing the downtown visitor's center from mid–May through mid–October. Alternatively, grab a taxi, ride a bike, walk, or take the Miacomet Loop bus. As the Cisco motto goes, "It's nice beer. If you can get to it."

Should you want to stay for a few days, visit *www.nantucket.net* or *www.nantucketchamber.org* for suggestions on where to eat, sleep, drink, and play. Many of the homes rebuilt in Nantucket's historic center after the Great Fire now serve as small hotels, inns, and luxury guest houses, but the luxurious White Elephant (50 Easton Street / *www.whiteelephanthotel.com*) is worth the splurge if you are in the mood for a romantic or posh getaway. This classic hotel sprawls along the harbor. Prime property, once lined with storehouses full of the whale oil that fueled the fire which consumed the city, is now engulfed in island charm, beautiful harbor vistas, fine food, and sophisticated comfort.

18

A WHALE OF A HOME

EASTHAM
– 1868 –

The remarkably well–preserved Victorian home of Captain Edward Penniman sits perched atop Fort Hill with views overlooking Eastham's marshlands and the white–capped Atlantic. It stands as a tribute to the extraordinary life of one of New England's most successful whaling captains. This wealthy, worldly Cape Codder made his fortune traversing the globe in pursuit of leviathans of the deep. By age fifty–three, Captain Penniman accumulated enough riches to retire anywhere in the world, but chose his beloved Eastham to build an opulent mansion for his family. The Penniman House, now a historic landmark in the care of the National Park Service, tells the true–life story of a man who voyaged around the world in pursuit of whales—while in his heart, he was never far from Cape Cod.

Edward Penniman was adamant in his belief that there was no lovelier place on earth than Eastham, the town in which he was born on August 16, 1831. Most Cape Cod fishermen had an early start to life at sea and Edward was no different. At age eleven he was working on a fishing vessel off the coast of Newfoundland, Canada; at twenty–one, he went on his first whaling expedition. Soon after, he became the captain of his own ship and chose the Massachusetts port of New Bedford as its home base. From here he launched seven whale hunts, which took him around the world, often for years at a time. He entered ports as far–flung as the Cape Verde Islands, New Zealand, Hawaii and the Arctic.

Penniman became fascinated with foreign cultures, collecting countless souvenirs during his journeys, but his regular letters home hinted that he preferred life with the family to being at sea. The extreme wealth attainable through a career in whaling could not be ignored given his penchant for adventure and a taste for the finer things in life. The Pennimans eventually decided to make the best of Edward's career choice by turning several of the whaling expeditions into family affairs. His wife and children accompanied him for three or four years, making the round–the–world voyages more tolerable. His wife, Betsy Augusta Penniman (whom he called "Gustie"), actually embraced life aboard the ship. She wrote in her memoirs that she enjoyed cooking and sewing, corresponding with friends back home, and developing her navigational skills.

The children also accompanied their parents on some of the whale hunts. A trip to the Arctic Ocean inspired their first son, Eugene, to follow in his father's footsteps to become a whaling ship captain. The Pennimans' youngest child, Neddie, went along on the second trip and entertained himself during the three-year journey by modeling wooden boats and sketching ships. The third and final trip included their thirteen-year-old daughter, Bessie, who had the opportunity to meet the Hawaiian royal family and who preferred sailing through warmer climates, such as Panama, San Francisco, and Hawaii. They were truly a worldly family.

In the 1860s the going rates for whale oil varied from $1.45 to $2.55 per gallon while whalebone sold for $15.80 per pound. Records indicate Penniman's ships carried thousands of barrels of whale oil and more than a hundred thousand pounds of whalebone. Do the math and it is easy to see how he amassed such a fortune. Captain Penniman became so successful in the whaling industry that he was able provide his family luxury unheard of by even the wealthiest of seamen. So, what should he do with all this money? Build a house, of course!

In 1868, after his fourth whaling expedition, Penniman returned to Eastham, purchased twelve acres of land from his father, and constructed an impressive home for himself and his family. He chose a site located on the west side of Town Cove, in the Fort Hill section of Eastham. This very narrow neck of Cape Cod is only about 3 miles wide between the Atlantic Ocean and Cape Cod Bay. Like any whaler of his time, Edward couldn't bear to be far from the sea, so he built a grand mansion on a windswept cliff overlooking the Atlantic.

Most of the Eastham residents lived in simple, conservative Cape Cod homes, but the worldly Pennimans had no qualms about building a modern, over-the-top home to showcase their treasures from around the globe. Well-versed in the most up-to-date architectural trends, Penniman commissioned his impressive home to be built in the

French Second Empire style. This sophisticated style, inspired by Napoleon III, was highly ornamental and included many architectural features, including mansard roofs such as one might find while strolling the grand boulevards of Paris.

The Pennimans' two–and–a–half–story, wood framed house has a colorful clapboard–exterior and steeply pitched mansard roof topped with red roof shingles. The new building must have been quite a site to his conservative neighbors. Captain Penniman spared no expense in building the most extravagant, modern house in Eastham, and possibly on the Cape. It wasn't the size, ornate details or elevated location that distinguished it from the simple homes of Cape Cod. The Penniman House was on the cutting edge of home technology and used the most contemporary techniques available at the time.

It was the first to have indoor plumbing. A rooftop collection system gathered water into an attic cistern from which gravity carries water down through pipes leading into the kitchen and bathroom. The heating and lighting systems of the home were also constantly updated as new technology evolved from using wood and coal fuel to kerosene and, eventually, electricity.

Inside and out, this unique home reveals how wealthy whaling families lived in the nineteenth century and this house in particular, reflects the tastes they developed after a lifetime of exposure to different world cultures. The rooms of the Penniman House were filled with imagination–stirring collections of artifacts, ranging from Arctic bear robes and European paintings to Nantucket scrimshaw.

Most symbolic of Edward Penniman's career is the thirteen–foot whale jawbone framing an entrance to the property, serving as a gateway. Passing between the whalebones is believed to bring good luck—and there is no doubt that Edward Penniman had a little bit of this in his lifetime. At age fifty–three, he retired as one of the most successful whaling captains in history.

Edward was finally able to sit back and enjoy the fruits of his labors by permanently retiring to his grand home on his beloved Fort Hill. More than a century later, the

Penniman House remains in a remarkable state of preservation. The floor plan is the same as it was in 1868, and most of the interior woodwork, finishes, hardware, and wall and ceiling coverings are original.

In recognition of the home's historical significance and its connection with the region's whaling era and this prestigious family, the Cape Cod National Seashore purchased the priceless property from Irma Penniman Broun, the captain's youngest granddaughter in the 1960s. Today, the Penniman House is a National Historic Site. Exhibitions of the family's written records, personal collections, and more than one hundred glass–plate pictures, taken between 1880 and 1913 by Captain Penniman's daughter Bessie, are on display. These eclectic collections of artifacts offer a glimpse into the Penniman's fascinating lives—and one of the most historically and architecturally important homes on Cape Cod.

EXPERIENCE

This Experience highlights 350 years of Cape Cod building. When someone refers to a "Cape Codder," the image that inevitably comes to mind is a traditional, gray shake–clad bungalow with pointy gables, high–pitched roofs and window boxes bursting with flowers. This particular style of home has its origins in the seventeenth century, when the earliest settlers lived in simple, sturdy homes able to withstand the harsh New England weather.

Cape Cod's best example of colonial residential architecture also happens to be one of Massachusetts's oldest houses. The Hoxie House (18 Water Street) in the village of Sandwich was built in 1675 for the town's second minister. The saltbox house was lived in (without electricity) until the 1950s and is now beautifully restored and preserved by the city. It is open for guided tours during the summer and fall, but even when it is closed, you can visit the property and see the exterior of the house. Right next door to the Hoxie House, also on Water Street, is the Dexter Grist Mill—one of the country's oldest water mill sites. Corn has been ground here since 1654 and the working mill continues to sell bags of cornmeal to help subsidize the maintenance of the gears and preservation of the building. Dexter Grist Mill is open for tours through the summer and fall.

The Cape Cod Colonial home remained popular throughout the region (and New England) until the early nineteenth century. A Greek Revival brought the addition of ancient classical architectural elements, such as columns, pilasters, and pediments to architectural design. Sandwich's Town Hall built in 1834 is a prime example of this style, as is the Barnstable County Courthouse on Main Street (Route 6A). The 1831 granite building sits just far enough back from the Old King's Highway, one might not notice that the columns are carved of wood fashioned to look like stone. But the best place to see an epic number of original Greek and Classical Revival homes is on Nantucket. A walk along Main Street transports you the days just after the island's Great Fire of 1846 (Read the previous story, *Nantucket Burning* for a detailed account). Rebuilding happened quickly and resulted in the highest concentration of pre–Civil War structures, most of which were built during this revival.

The restraint of classical architecture gave way to the embellished Victorian–era building. Captain Penniman's 1868 home falls into the colorful Victorian sub–category of French Second Empire. The home can be easily found at the intersection of Fort Hill and Governor Prence Roads in Eastham just off Route 6. It is open seasonally for tours and offers a look into the lives of this prominent whaling family.

From the sea captain's Victorian home, standing above the gateway to the Cape Cod National Sea Shore, we step into the twentieth century with a unique collection of more than 100 mid–century homes tucked into the landscape of the outer Cape. When the National Seashore was created in 1959, these homes were bought by the government and shortly after, most of them were abandoned and fell into disrepair. The Cape Cod Modern House Trust (*www.ccmht.org*) was established in 2007 as a grass roots non–profit organization to help protect and renovate these special houses deemed architecturally important. Three fully restored homes are now available for year round guest rental, guided tours, and artist or scholar residences. Purchasing the dazzling coffee table book, *Cape Cod Modern: Mid–century Architecture and Community on the Outer Cape* (by Peter McMahon and Christine Cipriani, 2014), helps support the ongoing efforts to maintain this important bit of architectural heritage, which like the Penniman House, will offer future generations a look into Cape Cod's lifestyle and culture of a previous century.

19

THE FRENCH CONNECTION

ORLEANS
– 1891 –

Have you ever wondered how news made its way around the world before cell phones and instant messaging, satellite dishes or cable television? Very slowly! Before the first transatlantic cable was laid in the late 1900s, word traveled only as fast as the horse or the ship carrying it. Communication between Europe and North America took upwards of a week, but that was considered reasonable for the time.

In 1891, the two continents were permanently connected via an underwater cable that ran between northern France and Cape Cod. The modest French Cable Station is located off Route 28 in Orleans. It houses the original communication equipment, which may seem primitive in this age. At the turn of the twentieth century, it was state–of–the–art technology.

The precedent for modern communication was set in the 1830s, when Professor Samuel F. B. Morse sent a message via Morse code from Baltimore to Washington. Within thirty years, historians recognized his magnetic telegraph as one of the most beneficial and innovative inventions of mankind. Telegraph lines appeared all over Europe and North America with messages being sent virtually instantaneously overland. Crossing water, however, presented a bit of a challenge.

Communication technology was in its infancy when, in 1845, the idea of a transatlantic cable was proposed. Scientists knew the underwater wires had to be heavily insulated and exceedingly strong to withstand the great depths of the Atlantic, but practical demonstrations proved it could be done. Two visionary British brothers, John and Jacob Brett, succeeded after several failed attempts in running a cable across the English Channel to France in 1851.

Five years later, the brothers joined an American named Cyrus Field in forming the Atlantic Telegraph Company. By June of 1857, 2,500 nautical miles of tough, waterproof cable had been manufactured. In August, the monstrous cable was loaded onto two ships and the formidable task of laying the transatlantic line began. Shortly into the journey, Cyrus Field and his engineers were taught a few very expensive lessons in trial and error.

Beginning in Valentia Harbor, Ireland, the ships sailed together into the Atlantic while slowly dropping the cable into the ocean. Everything seemed to be going as planned, but six days and 380 miles into the project, a wave crashed into one boat and the cable snapped. The ships were forced to return to port because there was not enough cable to continue on.

With high hopes—and another 700 feet of cable—a new approach was taken for connecting the two continents. On June 25, 1858, the same two ships met each other in the middle of the Atlantic and joined their respective ends of the cable. The ships began to sail in opposite directions back toward land but, the cable broke again! It continued to snap after the third and fourth attempts, so the engineers cut their losses and returned to Britain to regroup.

With just enough cable for one last ditch effort, the ships once again met in the mid–Atlantic and this time successfully laid the cable between Ireland and Newfoundland, Canada. On August 5, 1858, the two continents were officially connected—but this did not last for long! In less than a month, the high voltages used to send messages fried the underwater cables and communication ceased. It was back to the drawing board! More than two decades passed before another attempt was made.

In 1879, the Compagnie Française du Télégraphe de Paris à New York was formed with the sole purpose of laying a transatlantic cable. The company decided the cable should run between Brest, France, to St. Pierre in Canada's Miquelon Islands, then on to Eastham, Cape Cod. Using a cable manufactured in England by the Siemens Brothers and an enormous American ship, the USS *Faraday*, the cable was laid in less than four months. It stretched 2,242 nautical miles across the Atlantic to St. Pierre, Canada and continued another 827 nautical miles on to Cape Cod.

A large building was constructed in north Eastham to serve as a cable station for receiving messages from Europe and then transmitting them on to New York via an overland telegraph line. Surprisingly, the cable arrived on Cape Cod two weeks before the cable station was completed, so it was temporarily housed in the nearby

Nauset Beach Light keeper's house then later transferred.

After a short time, the station workers felt the Eastham location was inconvenient, so the cable company shifted its Cape Cod operation to Orleans, where they built the current French Cable Station in March of 1891. A connector cable was run from the old station at Nauset, across Nauset Marsh, to the new cable station in Orleans.

From this point on, technology advanced rapidly. Within seven years the cable, which came to be known as "*Le Direct*," totally bypassed Saint–Pierre and ran non–stop between Brittany, France, and Cape Cod, allowing instantaneous, two–way communication across the Atlantic for the first time—and it certainly came in handy! During its heyday, the French Cable Station played a vital role in transmitting information about a number of major international events. Many important messages were conveyed from the Orleans station.

In November 1898, the *Portland*, a steamship with 400 passengers aboard, sank in a battering winter gale. With wreckage and bodies washing ashore on Cape Cod, the French Cable Station was the first to transmit news to the world that there were no survivors. Due to the layout of the cables, the message had to be sent from Orleans to France then than relayed to New York. In less than five minutes news about the shipwreck made its way to America's major cities.

On May 31, 1927, it was befitting that news of another monumental transatlantic event was transmitted from the French Cable Station. From Cape Cod, the nation learned that Charles Lindbergh had made the first solo transatlantic crossing, flying the *Spirit of St. Louis* from New York to Paris.

This humble, little building also played an important role in both world wars. During World War I, the station was an essential lifeline between army headquarters in Washington, D.C. and the American forces in France. Marines guarded the cable station, which was used to send top–secret messages back and forth between the two countries.

The cable remained in operation throughout World War II, until France surrendered to Germany. In June 1940, an abrupt message arrived in Orleans reading, "Les Boches sont ici" (a derogatory message stating "the Germans are here!"). Immediately afterward, the cable went dead. The French end of the cable was now in the hands of the Nazis and both transmitters remained quiet throughout the rest of the war.

The cable hut in Orleans remained vacant long after the end of World War II, and despite more than 600 cables being laid around the world; the French Cable Station did not resume transmissions until 1952. Its second life, however, was to be short–lived. By the mid–twentieth century, telephone service had rendered the station obsolete, so it was forced to close its doors for good on November 24, 1959.

Inside the station, a faded 1959 calendar still hangs on the wall with November 26 heavily circled in pencil. The final message sent across the cable from Orleans read, "Have a happy Thanksgiving. Station closed," and the telegraph was shut down permanently.

EXPERIENCE

The French Cable Station (41 South Orleans Road, Orleans / www.frenchcablestationmuseum.org), which once served as a vital communication link between America and Europe stands today near Town Cove in Orleans. Visit the small, unique museum for a guided tour by knowledgeable docents. Time is well spent in this museum chock full of original communication equipment, educational displays about transmission and repairing cables, and educational videos. One of the more interesting artifacts is the Heurtley Magnifier, a machine that helped amplify weak signals from France and which is one of only three in existence.

The French Cable Station Museum is open to visitors most days during the summer and weekends in the fall. It is free of charge, but please leave a donation to help keep this interesting and vital piece of Cape Cod (and American) heritage maintained.

The next story in this book is also about telecommunications and how Cape Cod played a pivotal role in the first wireless trans–Atlantic message. If visiting Orleans in off–season or the French Cable Station happens to be closed, experience the early days of communication technology with a visit to the beach front spot where the Marconi Station once stood in South Wellfleet.

20
CONNECTING THE WORLD

SOUTH WELLFLEET
– 1903 –

A friendly banter between President and King went down in history as the first wireless two–way transatlantic telegraph message, tapped out in Morse code from Theodore Roosevelt to Edward VII, King of England.

TO:

HIS MAJESTY, EDWARD VII

London, Eng.

In taking advantage of the wonderful triumph of scientific research and ingenuity which has been achieved in perfecting a system of wireless telegraphy, I extend on behalf of the American People most cordial greetings and good wishes to you and to all the people of the British Empire.

THEODORE ROOSEVELT

Wellfleet, Mass., Jan. 19, 1903

TO:

The President,

White House, Washington, America

I thank you most sincerely for the kind message, which I have just received from you, through Marconi's trans–Atlantic wireless telegraphy. I sincerely reciprocate in the name of the British Empire the cordial greetings and friendly sentiment expressed by you on behalf of the American Nation, I heartily wish you and your country every possible prosperity.

EDWARD R. and I.

Sandringham, January 19, 1903

And so began worldwide radio communication from the shores of Cape Cod. The revolutionary technology underlying this exchange was not developed by an American, but by an Irish–Italian man, Guglielmo Marconi. His childhood dream of wireless communication was realized not in his homeland of Italy, in America.

By Marconi's own admission, he was not an inventor, nor was he ever formally educated in the sciences. In fact, the young man never performed well enough to be accepted to a university. What he had was deep pockets, family connections, and true entrepreneurial vision. His mother, Annie Marconi, was the daughter of the famed Andrew Jameson—Irish whiskey baron. Marconi grew up a persistent and privileged boy, with the finances to support his tireless experimenting with radio frequency.

By 1895, at age twenty–one, Marconi was finally able to piece together several existing bits of technology: a Morse code key, some batteries, an induction coil, a relay, a device for detecting radio waves called a "coherer," and his own personal invention, the "aerial and earth." His backyard experiments proved that this contraption could transmit messages via radio frequency as far as one and one–quarter mile—and through a hillside.

Marconi's intuitive vision of wireless communication between two points—through land masses, across water, and despite the curvature of the earth—using his transmitting device led him to do what any loyal Italian would do: offer the technology first to the Italian government. In typical bureaucratic fashion, the government dragged their feet too long, so in 1896 Marconi made his way to England. With a little help from family and friends in high places, his dream of sending a wireless signal across the Atlantic to North America would come to fruition.

In some ways, Marconi's lack of formal education contributed to his success. Many academics and scientists disagreed with his theory that radio waves could work beyond the horizon. With his unstoppable attitude he simply set out to prove that his instincts and notions were correct, rather than debate the skeptics. Through ongoing experiments (and a lot of family funding), Marconi demonstrated repeatedly that wireless transmission had the potential to compete with, if not supersede the cables that had been laid across the Atlantic. After successfully transmitting wireless messages from England to France across the English Channel, it was time to attempt the Atlantic.

In 1900, a high–powered transmitting station was built on the south coast of England, in the Cornwall village of Poldhu. From here, Marconi's team performed successful transmissions between England and Ireland. In 1901, Cape Cod was identified as the place to build America's first wireless station—but where along the Atlantic coast would the towers be erected?

Marconi settled on South Wellfleet after being denied the opportunity to build near the Highland Light at Truro and passing up the offer to place a station in the Barnstable area. As one of the highest points on the Cape, the towering cliff of South Wellfleet was a desirable location for its unobstructed transmission over the open sea. As Henry David Thoreau once described this area, it is a place "where a man may stand…and put all of America behind him." Wellfleet, located on the "wrist" of the Cape, was both a sensible and symbolic location.

Headquarters were set up in the Holbrook House in Wellfleet, and Marconi's men went to work building the towers. Despite storms toppling the aerials in Poldhu and a nor'easter blowing over the unsafe aerials in Cape Cod, Marconi persisted. The station in South Wellfleet was rebuilt with a better design and its transmitter building buzzed loud enough that it could be heard miles away—but the 20,000–volt transformer wasn't the only buzz around town.

Marconi rallied publicity for his new technology once he recognized the potential for extreme profit in a radio link between North America and Great Britain He convinced President Theodore Roosevelt to come to the station at South Wellfleet on January 18, 1903, to participate in the first ever two–way, transatlantic communication, with King Edward VII of England. The plan was to transmit the President's message to a station in Glace Bay, Nova Scotia, and then on to Poldhu, England. They would await response in the reverse order.

Roosevelt's message was tapped out in Morse code, but instead of receiving confirmation from the Canadian station confirming that the message had been sent on to England, they received a more pleasant surprise—an immediate and direct response from the King. The evening weather conditions were so clear that the message was picked up in Poldhu and the response transmitted directly back to Wellfleet, making it the first wireless telegram between America and Europe.

What began as simple transmissions from crude, timber towers in South Wellfleet quickly evolved into North America's primary "ship to shore" wireless communication center. Rising above skeptics and technical problems, Guglielmo Marconi bestowed radio upon the world and went on to win the 1909 Nobel Prize for his contribution. Radio and wireless technology has since become a radical scientific and social phenomenon, changing the face of the world's economy and culture.

EXPERIENCE

The coastline of towering dunes along South Wellfleet is impossibly beautiful, but challenged by constant erosion and deterioration. In 1903, this site was chosen for America's first power station because of its elevated location and exposure to the Atlantic—and for these exact reasons, Marconi's original power station no longer exists. Extreme cliff side erosion undermined both it and the 1970s interpretative center that stood until recently in its place.

The Marconi Station was closed in 1917 after being battered by several nor'easters, while the 1974 commemorative museum shelter met the wrecking ball in 2013. Plans for a new Marconi center are underway, but until it opens, visit the site and see a few bits of modern building material clinging precariously to the edge of the cliff. Between the interpretive signage, plaques and the windswept vistas over the Atlantic, one can easily imagine the zapping sounds of aerial towers and the mystique of sending messages across the waves to Europe.

If in Wellfleet between Memorial and Labor Day, head to legendary Beachcomber Bar and Restaurant perched overlooking the Atlantic. Enjoy food, music and great views of the surf crashing onto Cahoon Hollow Beach below. Maybe even knock back a shot of Jameson in honor of Mr. Marconi!

In the case of off–season visits, the Chatham Marconi Maritime Center (847 Orleans Road / *www.chathammarconi.org*) off Route 28 near Ryder's Cove is open year–round. The gentrified village of Chatham is currently associated with high–end shopping, flourishing arts, a dangerous coastline, and fabulous fish market but, the town's connection with early wireless communication technology may come as surprise. While Marconi's mammoth power station existed father north on the more prominent outcrop of South Wellfleet, Chatham was perfectly situated on the bend of the Cape for a highly sensitive receiving antennae to be built as part of a transmitting circuit to Norway. The Chatham campus was built in 1914 and after painstaking restoration throughout the 1990s was opened in 2003—just in time for the centennial celebration of the first transatlantic wireless transmission.

21

CUTTING THE CANAL

BOURNE
− 1914 −

When the Pilgrims first settled in Plymouth in 1621, the need for a passage across the neck of the Cape, between Cape Cod and Buzzards Bay, was apparent. Myles Standish and William Bradford were among the early colonists to discover the Manomet River drained west into Buzzards Bay, while less than a mile away, the Scusset River drained toward the east into Cape Cod Bay. These two men initiated a discussion to somehow connect the two tidal rivers, thus connecting two bays.

The General Court of Massachusetts formally spoke of building a canal through Barnstable as early as 1676, but little did they know this project would remain on the drawing board for 200 years. A century later, at the outbreak of the American Revolution, the state Assemblies were still talking about it. On June 10, 1776, George Washington sent an inquiry to Massachusetts's Governor James Bowdoin, about the potential of building a canal in the Cape Cod Bay area to help thwart British offenses. This inquiry led to the undertaking of the canal's first proper engineering survey but, no action was taken.

Throughout the early and mid–nineteenth century, many more surveys were conducted, and engineers gave favorable reports as to the possibility of a waterway being cut yet, none of the proposed projects moved forward. By 1860, the state decided to take on the task, but the outbreak of the Civil War once again caused a postponement of the project. The pressing need for a canal was clear as ships continually wrecked on the dangerous shoals and sandbars around the outer Cape.

After the end of the Civil War and the country began to stabilize, the Legislature of Massachusetts created a special charter incorporating a company called the Cape Cod Ship Canal Company. It was established on June 26, 1883, and was given until 1891 to complete what would become the largest canal in the world. Not surprisingly, struggles between the engineers, scientists, and financiers never allowed the project to get off the ground. During the years between 1891 and 1909 several companies attempted and failed to start or complete a canal. In the end, it would take a wealthy venture capitalist and twentieth century engineering to finally bring the Pilgrims' vision of a canal to fruition.

New York tycoon August Belmont, Jr., might be best known for creating Belmont Park, where the prestigious Belmont Races are held. But, if racehorses weren't a risky enough endeavor, Belmont spent most of his family fortune investing in two major mass transit projects—the New York City Subway and the Cape Cod Canal. In 1899 he purchased the Boston, Cape Cod, and New York Canal Company, which held the building charter for the Cape Cod Canal. Prominent civil engineer, William Barclay Parsons was hired as the project's chief engineer to conduct a feasibility study. Parsons' work on the New York City underground rapid transit system and his consulting role on the Panama Canal made him the ideal candidate to get the Cape Cod job done. On June 19, 1909, construction began.

The extreme difference in tides was the greatest geographical hurdle to overcome. The Cape Cod peninsula acts as a breaker for the Atlantic Ocean, slowing down the arrival of high tide into Cape Cod Bay. Because Buzzards Bay is less protected, high tide arrives here more than three hours earlier, while low tide sets in four hours earlier than in Barnstable on the bay side. At various times during the day, the water in Barnstable Bay can be 5.8 feet higher or 4.6 feet lower than the water in Buzzards Bay.

Conflicts arose as to whether or not to include locks, just in case the shallow end of the water might freeze. Heated debates were held to determine what type of profit might be expected, the level of maintenance required over time, and the overall practicality of a canal across Cape Cod. The decision was made to dig the canal to depths that would accommodate the variations in the tides rather than build locks.

For two years, a fleet of twenty–six vessels and several crews of workers dredged inland from the east and the west, intending to meet in the middle. Work was unexpectedly delayed for three years as steam shovels were unable to move massive granite boulders formed during the last ice age. Slow progress was unacceptable to Belmont. He was absolutely adamant about the Cape Cod Canal opening before the Panama

Canal. The three bridges built to span the canal, Buzzards Bay Railroad Bridge, and the Bourne and Sagamore vehicular drawbridges, were all completed by 1912. This added additional pressure to bring the project up to speed. Extra digging machines were brought in and hardhat divers were sent to shatter the boulders with dynamite. In a short time, the project was back on track.

By the spring of 1914, an impressive waterway cut through the seven miles of land, slicing Cape Cod peninsula off from the mainland at its shoulder. The Cape was officially an island. A single dam separated Buzzards Bay from Cape Cod Bay. Belmont and Parsons held a ceremony in celebration of its near–finish where they bottled the blended waters of the two bays and opened the final sluiceway.

The Cape Cod Canal officially opened on July 29, 1914. A parade of ships, including Belmont's private yacht and the *McDougall* (a US Navy destroyer carrying Franklin Delano Roosevelt, who was Assistant Secretary of the Navy at the time), made the journey through the new privately operated toll canal. A long–term passage between the two bays was finally established. Belmont not only completed what so many before him had failed to do, he achieved his objective of opening Cape Cod's canal seventeen days before the Panama Canal.

What did not live up to expectations was the amount of profit the canal would generate. Tolls were expensive and the passage was narrow, so even if a captain could afford the rates, his boat might not fit in the canal. Many mariners continued to use the Atlantic coastal routes and the canal changed hands a few times since opening. Today, the Cape Cod Canal remains to be the widest sea–level canal in the world and since has become one of the region's most memorable and impressive geographic features.

EXPERIENCE

One of the most nostalgic moments of visiting Cape Cod is crossing high above the canal on the Bourne or Sagamore Bridges while watching the mainland shrink into the rear view mirror. Big boats look like tiny specks in the blue water as the canal meanders off to the east and west. Part of this experience is often sitting in gridlocked traffic, especially during peak season (from Memorial Day through Labor Day) when weekenders arrive *en masse* on Friday evening and make a slow–moving exodus on Sunday afternoons. Try to avoid these particular time frames by visiting during shoulder–season or arriving and departing at unusual times of the week, otherwise, come armed with patience.

Once situated on the Cape, abandon the automobile and hop on your bike. Whether traveling with bicycles in tow or renting one, there is no shortage of trails for all skill sets, ranging from easy paved paths to rugged hilly trails. The Cape Cod Canal Bikeway managed by the U.S. Army Corps of Engineers is a fairly flat, recreational trail running along the shoreline on both sides of the canal. The wide, family–friendly paths are designed for non–motorized vehicles and pedestrians. A leisurely peddle (or run) along the south side of the canal takes you approximately seven miles between the Bourne and Sagamore Bridges. Lovely perspectives of the water, boat traffic, stunning bridge architecture, and a few historic sites like Aptucxet Trading Post (see Chapter 7) are found along the way. It is often windy along the canal, so keep in mind you might have the wind to your back in one direction, but will have to peddle into it the opposite way.

The online list at *www.capecodbikeguide.com* is a good source of trail information, maps, driving directions, difficulty levels, and other parking and restroom practicalities. To experience another side of Cape Cod via bicycle, hit the Rail Trail, which follows 22 miles along the former Old Colony Railway, from South Dennis to South Wellfleet. This popular trail is well maintained and extremely busy for a reason as it leads along quaint little villages, breathtaking beaches, coastal overlooks, and foggy cranberry bogs. Some sections are more rigorous than the Cape Cod Canal Bikeway. Read up on the trailheads, difficulty level, parking, and traffic crossings online at *www.traillink.com*. Remember during peak season, the parking at trailheads may be at a premium so have a back up plan in place. If renting bikes on the Cape, consult *www.capecodvisitorsdirectory.com* for a comprehensive list of rental services all over the Cape and Islands.

22

ASSAULT IN AMERICAN WATERS

ORLEANS
– 1918 –

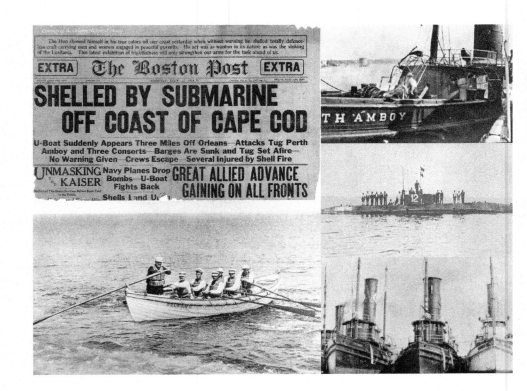

The town of Orleans endured many attacks throughout the country's early wars since its incorporation in 1797. When local militia repelled the British ship *Newcastle* during the War of 1812 (as told in the previous story: *Keeping the British At Bay*) more than a century of peaceful existence followed—until the summer of 1918, when a German U–boat surfaced and fired on Orleans. This was the only town in the United States directly attacked during World War I.

Submarine development began in the 1860s, but the concept of underwater military machines became a reality when Rudolph Diesel introduced an engine to power submarines in 1895. The United States, England, France, Germany, and Russia all had advanced submarine technology in their possession by the onset of World War I in 1914.

On the morning of Sunday July 21, 1918, the residents of Orleans were going about business as usual—attending church, fishing, and relaxing. Tourists were lazing away the summer in seaside cottages. Even the tugboat *Perth Amboy*, with its four barges was crawling at a leisurely Sunday pace along the Nauset shoreline.

Despite the calm normalcy of east coast America, there existed a few not–so–subtle reminders that much of the world was in the middle of a Great War. French ships guarded the transatlantic cables that had recently been laid between Orleans and France. An airbase was built in Chatham, just down the coast from where the Coast Guard diligently patrolled the waters. Nearby shipyards and arms manufacturers were increasing production. The Americans' contribution to the war effort came in the form of ammunition, soldiers, and supplies that were shipped overseas. Cape Codders were cognizant of the wartime traffic sailing past their front door.

Beginning with the sinking of the *Lusitania* off the coast of Ireland in 1915, the Germans made it very clear that they intended to use the new submarine technology to stop the Americans from supplying the Allies. The following year, the United States became increasingly aware of the capabilities of the German submarines. Several German U–boats made impromptu visits to major East Coast cities, including

Baltimore and Newport, under the pretense of doing business. The underlying message: German submarines could penetrate American waters.

In late 1916, a German submarine cruised through Narragansett Bay Naval Station in Rhode Island, sailed off into the Atlantic, and promptly sank one Dutch and four British ships. Around this same time, the United States began shoring up her coastal defenses. Steel nets were installed across the entrances to major harbors and naval air stations were built to aid in the detection and destruction of enemy submarines.

The United States remained neutral until it was forced into the conflict when Germany unleashed its submarine force in 1917. Any of their enemies' ships, not just military, found in International waters were considered fair game. German U-boats attacked American vessels all over the Atlantic, sinking six civilian merchant ships near Nantucket. In a short period of time, many civilian and merchant ships ended up at the bottom of the ocean. The Great War was hitting close to home.

The United States joined forces with the Western Allies on April 6, 1917. The New England coast remained U-boat-free for a year, but naval commanders knew the Germans might turn their military attentions toward America at any moment. That time came on June 14, 1918. A single German submarine, with a crew of seventy-eight, was deployed to American waters. The German U-156 sank one British and two Norwegian ships while on its way to lay mines in the New York harbor. On July 19, one of its mines sank a 14,000-ton cruiser, the *USS San Diego.* Before the *San Diego* had even settled to the ocean floor near Long Island, the U-156 was on its way to wreak havoc along the Cape Cod coast.

The morning of July 21, 1918, was no different than any other in Orleans—until the first shot rang out from the attacking vessel. Onlookers were horrified as the stealth U-156 surfaced and began firing rounds into the *Perth Amboy* and her four barges. A torpedo made a direct hit to the tugboat setting it ablaze. In all, an estimated 146 rounds were fired into the four boats—one shell even made it onto the beach.

A dazed Coast Guardsman scrambled up the tower of the station to get a better view of Nauset Harbor, uncertain of what was happening. Finally realizing that a German submarine was firing on Orleans, he radioed the naval air station in Chatham to report the American mainland was under attack.

As the U–156 continued its assault, other Coast Guardsmen set out in lifeboats to rescue thirty–two people from the burning boats, including the Captain, his wife and children. The heroes rowed directly into the steady line of fire and eventually carried everyone to safety. Before the U–boat could submerge, military seaplanes from Chatham Naval Air Base arrived and dropped bombs that failed to explode. The Germans slipped away before the navy launched a more effective counter–attack.

The confrontation with the U–boat succeeded in frightening the American public who dubbed this one–sided incident the "Battle of Orleans." Many more enemy submarines followed the U–156 across the Atlantic, sinking more than ninety vessels between Newfoundland and North Carolina. The Allies' successful anti–submarine campaign eventually brought an end to the menacing German U–boats.

EXPERIENCE

Little tangible evidence of the Battle of Orleans survives today, other than the rusting bits of sunken barges off Nauset Beach, along with a few frantic telegrams between an Orleans resident and the *Boston Globe* claiming that Orleans had been attacked. This correspondence is currently in the possession of the Orleans Historical Society (3 River Road / *www.orleanshistoricalsociety.org*). The Society's museum collections, held in a historic landmarked Greek Revival Meeting House, celebrate the town's rich heritage through Colonial and Native American artifacts, history–themed events, and genealogical records.

A more peaceful approach to experiencing this unusual bit of military history is to take a tranquil cruise around the marshes, estuaries, and islands of Little Pleasant Bay or Nauset Harbor by kayak or canoe. It's not exactly a submarine, but you can still navigate watery turns through the marsh grass, watching for birds, fish, crabs, and other wildlife. If bringing your own boat, consult the Orleans, Chatham, or Eastham town Websites for information about launch areas. Also, be sure to check the tidal charts since this low–lying, narrow section of the Cape sometimes converges with the Atlantic Ocean, causing a bit of a stir in the marshes. If a guided expedition is preferred, contact Cape Kayaking (*www.capekayaking.com*) who can provide knowledgeable guides to conduct a variety of thoughtful tours in and around the Cape Cod National Seashore.

The ten–mile finger of Nauset Beach (not to be confused with the more northerly Nauset Light Beach associated with the lighthouse) stretches from Orleans all the way south to Chatham, providing plenty of opportunity to catch the same beautiful vistas of the Atlantic Ocean that the fine folks of Orleans had a century ago.

23

A BRIDGE IS
RE-BOURNE

BOURNE
– 1935 –

One of the most important events in Bourne's town history is not so much the opening of the Cape Cod Canal, but the completion of the Bourne Bridge three years earlier. While the canal was under construction, a railroad bridge and two cantilever drawbridges were concurrently being built—all of which were completed well before there was a canal to cross. At the west end of the Cape, Buzzards Bay Railroad Bridge was completed in 1910 and Bourne's drawbridge was finished in 1911. The Sagamore Bridge at the east end was finished in 1912.

The Cape Cod Canal was an instant success when it opened on July 29, 1914. Shipping times between the regions north and south of the Cape were improved and tourists began pouring onto Cape Cod. The Bourne Bridge accommodated cars and trolleys providing public transport between Monument Beach on the Cape and New Bedford on the mainland. The bridges could only be crossed when there was no marine traffic so, automobiles going to and from the Cape experienced long waits—not unlike today!

Boats also experienced delays. The drawbridge only opened to a width of 140 feet limiting the size of the vessels that could pass through. Developers realized after just a few years that the canal was not generating the type of revenue that had been projected. Canal financier and famed racehorse breeder, August Belmont, Jr. footed the bill to deepen the canal, which increased boat traffic, but it was still not as profitable as predicted.

When a German submarine sunk a tugboat off the shore of Nauset a few years later on July 21, 1918, the canal became an issue of national security. With little objection from business–minded Belmont, the United States government under President Woodrow Wilson's direction purchased the canal for $11.5 million. In 1928, the Army Corps of Engineers took over responsibility of maintaining the canal and its three bridges, which they continue to do to this day.

While the canal may not have brought huge prosperity to the Cape's upper towns as expected, improvements to the canal and bridges created 2,100 valuable jobs during the Great Depression. In 1933, the Public Works Administration (PWA) authorized the updating and reconstruction the three canal bridges. The Boston architectural firm of Cram and Ferguson redesigned the bridges while Fay, Spofford, and Thorndike of Boston supervised construction. Whenever possible, manual labor was used in place of machinery to help generate employment opportunities, as dangerous as it might have been.

The canal was widened to 500 feet and deepened to 32 feet. The foundations for two new highway bridges were laid in December of 1933. The Sagamore Bridge crossed from the mainland of Massachusetts onto the Cape at Sandwich near the eastern terminus of the canal. The Bourne Bridge was constructed approximately two miles from the western end near Buzzards Bay. Two years and $40 million later, the canal and bridges were finally modernized and improved.

The Bourne and Sagamore Bridges are mirror images of each other. The high roads arch gracefully over the canal, each designed for four lanes of cars without impeding the water traffic below. The elevated bridges provide vessels with a vertical clearance of 135 feet above water and a horizontal clearance of 480 feet.

The two structures differ from one another in that the Bourne Bridge is 2,384 feet long, almost 1,000 feet longer than the Sagamore Bridge. The Bourne Bridge received critical acclaim prior to opening. It was awarded the American Institute of Steel Construction's Award of Merit as "The Most Beautiful Bridge Built During 1934,"—recognizing it as one of the country's most significant and innovative steel bridges of the time.

The Bourne and Sagamore Bridges were dedicated together on June 22, 1935, with lavish ceremonies and aerial shows. A parade consisting of 8,000 people crossed over both bridges and marched for seven-and-a-half miles along the south side of the canal, entertaining an impressive 200,000 onlookers. Massachusetts' Governor James Michael Curley performed the ribbon cutting at the Bourne Bridge, while Eleanor Robson Belmont, widow of August Belmont, Jr., cut the ribbon at the Sagamore Bridge.

Today, more than 35 million vehicles per year pass over the two bridges, which provide the only land links between Cape Cod and mainland Massachusetts.

EXPERIENCE

There is no better way to experience the cape than by exploring at a leisurely pace. Take your time driving the 160-mile circuit beginning at the Sagamore Bridge, following the coastline of the Cape and ending at the Bourne Bridge. Slow travel may not be the most appealing prospect in the middle of peak summer when bumper-to-bumper traffic already moves at a snail's pace. But, there is something to be said about hopping in your car and setting out to discover a new beach, harbor or clam shack.

Shoulder season, which is May and September, is the best time to casually travel around the Cape. The crowds are thin while the seasonal businesses are open. Spring and fall often brings "Chamber of Commerce" weather and postcard perfect beach days—with the added bonus of free beach parking lots.

Cross over the canal using the Sagamore Bridge, bypassing the major artery of Route 6 for the slower, more scenic drive along Route 6A, also known as Old King's Highway. Several points of interest related to the canal and bridge history are located along the waterway on either side of the canal. The only part of the original Bourne Bridge that still exists is a large concrete wall, which was the old bridge abutment. It is located to the west of the present-day bridge on the north side of the canal.

Follow Route 6A from Sandwich along the contour of the Bay all the way into Provincetown. This two-lane road leads through the scenic villages of the Upper, Mid and Lower Cape, before taking the turn north and eventually merging with the Highway Route 6 at the distinctive Orleans roundabout.

The scenery and population changes dramatically upon entering the protected portion of the Cape Cod National Seashore. The landscape feels a little more rugged and untamed, even though the towns of Eastham, Wellfleet, and Truro have busy, little town centers. The Outer Cape provides the quintessential Cape Cod seaside experience for many visitors.

This portion of the road trip ends when Route 6 and 6A once again split at Truro, and 6A carries on as a coastal road along Cape Cod Bay into Provincetown. Restaurants, shops, galleries, markets, harbors, clam shacks, and beaches line the stretch of highway along the 6A stretch of highway.

Route 6 and 6A converge in wild and wacky P'Town. Cape Cod's most vibrant, artsy, kooky, fun village is situated on the sandy tip of Cape Cod. It is a visit for its great history, interesting architecture, Portuguese and fishing heritage, bustling waterfront, wonderful restaurants, and art galleries. Provincetown was put on the cultural map when artists, writers, actors, and other creative types began taking up residence here in the nineteenth century. While retaining a strong arts community, Provincetown is even more popular as a destination spot for LGBT tourists. The incredibly flamboyant and colorful town is worth a visit, whether gay or straight, artsy or not. Provincetown is such a unique place unlike anywhere else.

Leaving P'Town, follow Route 6 south, along the Atlantic shoreline back through Truro, South Wellfleet, Eastham, and Orleans. Take time for hiking or biking the hilly Province Lands dunes, kayaking through the Great Marsh, or basking on gorgeous sweeps of protected beaches against the backdrop of towering, 100–foot sand dunes. John F. Kennedy passed legislation to protect this region when creating the Cape Cod National Seashore in 1961. Read more about this area in the story, *Down By the Seashore*.

When you reach the Orleans roundabout, follow Route 28 south toward Chatham. This long, winding road runs along the south coast from Orleans through the Lower, Mid and Upper Cape, all the way back to the Bourne Bridge. Route 28 is also referred to as Main Street, passing through the towns of Chatham, Harwich Port, Dennis Port, South and West Yarmouth, then through the sprawling center of Hyannis.

Hyannis is a large town where shopping malls, ferries, and restaurants carry on with business—as—usual year—round. Route 28 maintains a distinctly commercial vibe in neighboring Centerville, before making a southerly turn through Mashpee and Osterville, down around the jetty of land at Falmouth. Follow 28 north along Buzzards Bay where Pocasset and Monument Beaches are particularly popular with sailors and families for its convenient location near the bridges and canal. Route 28 ends as it crosses the Bourne Bridge to mainland Massachusetts.

This bridge—to—bridge road trip can be driven in the opposite direction from Bourne to Sandwich, too. If pressed for time, but still with an urge to explore, hop on the highway (Route 6) to bypass a section of the slow road. No matter which part of the Cape you prefer, or whatever time of year you visit, get out and see something new. Cape Cod is diverse in its geography, history, waterfront, and scenery. It is surprisingly bigger than one might expect. There are hidden gems to be found during every visit. So, grab a map (or your GPS), hop on your bike or in a car, and just slow down; savor the journey.

24

GRAVEYARD OF
THE ATLANTIC

CHATHAM
– 1952 –

In the wee, dark hours of a frigid February morning, the uncanny alignment of a full-scale nor'easter and two unsuspecting tankers culminated into a chilling tale of two doomed ships, each ripped in half and awaiting what seemed an impossible rescue. On February 18, 1952, the SS *Pendleton* was bound for Boston, while the *Fort Mercer* was headed for Portland, Maine. These two World War II–era tankers of nearly identical design, carrying identical cargo, were being volleyed over 60-foot waves in the same crippling storm. If that isn't eerie enough, both boats cracked completely in half within a few hours of each other. Four ragged halves of the two ships were thrashed about in the waves for a full day and night off the coast of Chatham. The parallel calamities of both ships resulted in the greatest U.S. Coast Guard rescue of all time.

The *Pendleton* was due to dock in Boston at dawn on February 18, but poor visibility made it impossible to sail into the harbor. Captain John Fitzgerald was forced to turn the ship back out into Massachusetts Bay to ride out the storm. Wind and sea conditions only worsened and at 5:50 a.m., with no warning other than a few violent lurches, the *Pendleton* split in half between its two cargo tanks. The captain and seven officers were stranded in the bow (the front section of the boat), while thirty-three engineers and crew members were stuck on the stern (the back half of the boat). Crewman, Fred Brown said the noise was "like the tearing of a large piece of tin… a noise that sends shivers up and down the spine and jangles every nerve."

Unfortunately, the radio was in the front of the ship while the engine and power were in the back, severing any chance of communication with the Coast Guard. An S.O.S. signal was unable to be sent. If there was any upshot to being trapped in the rear portion of the ship, it was that the crew could steer their half of the boat with the remaining power. The officers up front were not as fortunate. With no electricity in the bow, they were left powerless at the mercy of gale-force winds, horizontal frozen rain, and sixty-foot waves. Both pieces of ship drifted for forty miles in the mountainous seas, ending up just a few miles off the coast of Chatham.

As no distress signal was issued, nearly eight hours passed before the Chatham Lifeboat Station picked up the *Pendleton* on its radar screen—they noticed the ship was well off its normal course. More perplexing was why the signal showed up in two blips rather than one. The situation was about to get even more complicated. While the broken *Pendleton* languished less than six miles off the coast of Chatham, the *Fort Mercer* was suffering the same grim fate 37 miles farther out.

In the early morning hours, while the *Pendleton* turned back to the sea, the *Fort Mercer* was encountering the same rough conditions. A few hours after the *Pendleton* cracked in half and while its crew was enduring the merciless elements, the *Fort Mercer* was about to lead a somewhat parallel life, but with one distinct difference. The *Fort Mercer* was able to transmit an S.O.S. to the Coast Guard before breaking up. This was to be the saving grace for both ships!

After hearing a horrifying cracking sound at 8:00 a.m., Captain Frederick Paetzel immediately alerted the crew and contacted the Coast Guard that an emergency situation was at hand. Cutters were alerted but had to travel from Nantucket. By no means were they close, but a rescue effort was under way. At 10:30 a.m., the *Fort Mercer* was still in one piece, but by noon it had cracked and was spurting oil. At 12:03 p.m., the captain issued the final distress call, "hull splitting," and shared their stormy location as 37 miles east of Chatham. Seven minutes later, the ship broke in two and communication went dead. Similar to the *Pendleton*, nine officers were trapped up front without power while thirty–four crewmen were in the back trying to keep the rear end afloat.

The Coast Guard dispatched five cutters, two lifeboats, and numerous aircraft in the direction of the *Fort Mercer*, still unaware that the *Pendleton* disaster was simultaneously unfolding closer to Chatham's dangerous, shallow shoreline. In addition to the ability to issue a distress call, the *Fort Mercer* luckily was in deeper water. This offered another ray of hope to ride out the storm as the waves did not batter the broken boat as brutally as they did the *Pendleton* in shallower water. The drawback to being farther out is that it took the Coast Guard a lot longer reach the ship. Still, the cutters made slow progress, and eventually came upon both halves of the *Fort Mercer*.

Rescue attempts lasted well into the next day. The massive icebreakers, *Acushnet* and *Eastwind* finally arrived at the stern of the *Fort Mercer*, but neither were suited to draw alongside of the violently bobbing bits of vessel with its human cargo. A few men were recovered by running rubber rafts on lines between the boats, but this posed too much of a risk. The heaving and rolling of the two large ships created roller–coaster–like conditions for those in the rafts. The *Acushnet* managed a daring maneuver by backing in dangerously close to the *Fort Mercer*, allowing eighteen men to jump to safety. Thirteen others remained behind because of injury, age or the need for their expertise to continue steering the half–ship.

While rescue efforts continued at the stern, the Coast Guard cutter *Yakutat* discovered the bow section of the *Fort Mercer* around 6:00 p.m., but spent most of the night unsuccessfully trying to put a transfer line aboard. Knowing they could not be retrieved from the ship's bridge, the crew of the *Fort Mercer* devised a plan to tie flags together and lower themselves onto a more protected area of the ship where there were greater possibilities of rescue. More than twenty hours after the *Fort Mercer* had been ripped apart, a final effort was made to rescue the four remaining survivors amid thirty–five–foot swells, freezing horizontal rain, and fifty–knot winds.

A lifeboat and rubber rafts were launched under extremely dangerous conditions. Due to the captain's ailments, the crew wanted him to go first. Despite his insistence on staying with the ship, he jumped and was plucked from the waves after floundering for a minute in the icy water. The final three men were rescued a few minutes before the bow capsized. Twenty hours after this horrific saga began, 38 out of 43 crewmen were saved from the *Fort Mercer,* which was a slightly better outcome than for those on the *Pendleton.*

Sometime during this sequence of rescue operations, a Coast Guard aircraft went searching for the *Fort Mercer*'s lifeboats and issued a report that he had spotted the bow of a ship, rolling in the surf just off the coast of Chatham. How could this be? It was broadcasted that rescuers were already on the scene, plucking survivors from the bow of the *Fort Mercer*, but there was no aircraft or ships in sight of this vessel. When asked his position, the pilot turned out to be 50 miles away from the said rescue scene. He flew in to get a closer look and read the name on the bow. This was the surprising first sighting of the *Pendleton*—at least one half of it.

The lifeboat station captain was in disbelief, as was the rest of the Coast Guard. It all came clear that they were dealing with two shipwrecks of the same magnitude, and their hands were already full with one. Radar operators at the Chatham Lifeboat Station now had the bow of the *Pendleton* in sight. They knew the second unidentified bleep on the radar had to be its stern, but it was drifting rapidly to the south, directly for the shallow, shifting Chatham Bar where it was in danger of capsizing and being dashed into pieces.

The rescue cutters that were diverted to the *Pendleton* could not move in close enough to make a rescue attempt because of the dangerous shifting sandbars. The men on board the cutters watched helplessly as the lone survivor jumped into the sea too soon to be rescued. By the time smaller lifeboats could get to the bow of the *Pendleton*, the ravaging storm had claimed the lives of all eight officers who had been aboard this part of the boat.

A rescue operation was simultaneously underway for the back half of the *Pendleton*, which was being monitored by radar. Chief Engineer Raymond Sybert had been steering the stern of the *Pendleton* using an emergency rudder control, trying not to run aground. The crew had a portable radio and listened to reports of the *Fort Mercer* rescue, but they feared the Coast Guard was not aware of their own dire straits. Hope was renewed when they learned a lifeboat was launched from Chatham Lifeboat Station—for them! But it was not going to be an easy task, even though they were just a few miles out.

Four courageous men in a thirty–six–foot, wooden lifeboat with a ninety–horsepower engine laboriously motored out over the notorious Chatham Bar into conditions often compared to those in the movie *A Perfect Storm*. They knew the odds were stacked against them. Moving mountains of water shattered windows, wrenched the compass from its mount, and drove the boat over sixty and seventy–foot waves into the black abyss of the Atlantic. These men went bravely forward with selfless heroism, potentially facing their own deaths —and without a compass.

The crew navigated with little more than dead reckoning and a good ear through thundering seas to the *Pendleton's* stern. Chillingly, the lifeboat captain could see nothing, but he could hear the creaking of the hull and the sounds of metal being pounded by waves. The sailors stranded on the *Pendleton* clung to hope and watched, spellbound, as the spotlight of the little lifeboat drew closer and closer; its engine occasionally dying out and sputtering back to life as it roller–coastered over frothy waves. An aircraft circled overhead while flares lit the violent scene. Coast Guard cutters sat off in deeper water unable to help as each man climbed, one–by–one, down a rope ladder from the stern of the *Pendleton* onto the rescue boat. Sadly one person, George "Tiny" Myers, was lost in the waves, but in the end 32 of the 33 on the stern were rescued. With 36 frozen, waterlogged, weary men crammed aboard, the tiny, wooden boat precariously made its way back to the shores of Chatham. The four volunteer crewmen of the lifeboat were awarded the Coast Guard's Gold Lifesaving Medal, comparable to a Congressional Medal of Honor—a well–deserved recognition for their outstanding navigational skills and disregarding their own safety to rescue fellow seamen from imminent death.

Amid 20 hours of hurricane–force winds, sixty–foot waves, snow squalls, and often in pitch–blackness, 32 of the 41 crew members were rescued from the *Pendleton,* and 38 of 43 crew members were saved from the *Fort Mercer.* These extraordinary feats of seamanship have gone down as two of the most dramatic rescues in the 214–year history of the United States Coast Guard. In all, five gold life–saving medals, four silver life–saving medals, and fifteen commendation medals were awarded—for a total of 24 citations for heroism during the rescues.

Until 1978, the *Pendleton's* rusting hulk was visible above the waters east of Monomoy Island, posing little threat to navigation. That winter's great blizzard submerged the structure forcing the Coast Guard to demolish what suddenly became a navigational hazard. Today, twisted wreckage and large machinery, including the ships generator, rises to within 25 feet of the surface. The stern of the *Pendleton* rests off Chatham Bar as a headstone for all those who lost their lives in the Graveyard of the Atlantic during this unparalleled double shipwreck. It also remains a haunting reminder of the old Coast Guard adage: "You have to go out, but you don't have to come back."

EXPERIENCE

Anyone who has spent time on "the elbow" of Cape Cod knows well the moodiness of the Chatham coastline. Even on the sunniest of days, fog might roll in like a ghost, cloaking the beach in a mist that makes visibility near impossible. Then it vanishes as quickly as it appeared. The water is moody too. Sandbars peek above the shallow, choppy water, as do seals and sharks. A stroll along the beach makes it easy to imagine both the romance and challenge of having to navigate this section of the Atlantic, where storms are constantly rearranging the landscape, attaching sand bars to the mainland or creating new openings between sandy spits out to the sea.

It is no wonder this area has been dubbed "The Graveyard of the Atlantic" as 3,000 documented shipwrecks lie off the coast between Chatham and Truro, including the *Pendelton* and *Fort Mercer*. It is scenic, treacherous and magnificent all at once. Ironically, for as populated as Chatham becomes in high season, some of Cape Cod's wildest and uninhabited parts are just a few miles south, along the eight–mile sandy finger of land forming the barrier islands of North and South Monomoy. The 7,600 acre Monomoy National Wildlife Refuge (Wikis Way, Morris Island, Chatham / www.fws.gov/refuge/Monomoy) was established in 1944 to protect the sensitive habitats of marshlands, dunes, and ponds that attract migratory sea, shore, and water birds. Colonies of gray and harbor seals also call this home, which inevitably attracts sharks into the area. There is a reason why the cove between North and South Monomoy Island is named Shark Hole. There is no electricity, no paved roads and no human habitation in the refuge, which encourages more than 285 species of migratory birds to rest, nest and feed here.

The quickest way to visit the remote island is on a guided tour with one of a few outfitters who run seasonal fishing excursions, seal and whale watching trips to the islands. Rip Ryder Monomoy Island Ferry (Wikis Way, Chatham / www.monomoyislandferry.com) has been in business for about 25 years and offers Seal Cruises along the west side of the islands from May through October. During the cruise you could see thousands of seals in their natural habitat before taking a guided walking tour of South Monomoy Island. A family or group of friends may consider booking a private boat trip to South Monomoy for an in–depth wildlife sighting tour and walk out to the lighthouse. These tours leave from the Monomoy Wildlife Refuge Center, which is worth a visit, whether you are taking a tour or not.

Monomoy Seal Cruise (702 Route 28 / www.monomoysealcruise.com), out of Harwich Port, sails along Nantucket Sound, making stops at a few scenic harbors, while an on–board naturalist narrates during the one and a half hour tour to the Monomoy Islands. Being aboard a boat lends a new appreciation of what sailors and fishermen have contended with on a daily basis through the centuries.

If a boat ride to Monomoy is out of the question (or if it is off–season), harbor seals can usually be found stalking the fishing boats as they arrive with their haul at the Chatham Fish Pier (Barcliff Avenue). Who says there's no such thing as a free lunch? Whether the seals are considered a nuisance or a tourist attraction, the playful creatures float and dive around the boats, feeding on fish either dropped or snatched from the nets—and posing for pictures.

To visit the Monomoy Islands by foot requires a lot more planning with food, water and sturdy footwear, plus an absolute awareness of the tidal charts. The least strenuous waterfront walk is an easy one–mile loop from the Monomoy Wildlife Refuge Center on Morris Island (not really Monomoy, but still part of the Refuge) along the beach and through some of the island scrub back to the trailhead. This is perfect for anyone just wanting a taste of adventure and some outdoor exercise. For the sturdier outdoors person, try the ten–mile round trip trek from the Chatham Light, along the squishy tidal flats of South Beach, and around the perimeter of Morris Island to Harding Point overlooking Stage Harbor. While neither hike is on the Monomoy Islands proper, there is no shortage of wildlife sightings, close encounters with tidal pools, waves, and beautiful dunes.

The hike to North or South Monomoy Island is a very long, but rewarding experience. The 18 mile round-trip trek beginning at the Chatham Light and leading out to the tip of South Monomoy is not for the faint of heart. Be sure to consult with the Refuge Center (508–945–0594), which has the final word on what areas of the islands are opened or closed based on weather, migrating wildlife, or other hazards. A word of caution: don't mess with the flora or fauna. If a seal (or a hundred) is basking on the beach, keep your distance. No matter how cute they look, wild animals might bite. Not to mention, they weigh upward of 300 pounds. Otherwise, this unique park was created as part of the National Wildlife Refuge System to protect animals and their natural habitat, while allowing us to enjoy it.

Whether exploring on foot or by boat, the coastline around Chatham, Morris and Monomoy Islands presents us with a clear idea as to why the elbow of the Cape has a reputation for perilous journeys just beyond the bar.

25

DOWN BY THE SEASHORE

CHATHAM TO PROVINCETOWN
– 1961 –

"But this shore will never be more attractive than it is now. Such beaches as are fashionable are here made and unmade in a day, I may almost say, by the sea shifting its sands. What are springs and waterfalls? Here is the spring of springs, the waterfall of waterfalls. A storm in the fall or winter is the time to visit it; a lighthouse or a fisherman's hut the true hotel. A man may stand there and put all America behind him."

—Henry David Thoreau, *Cape Cod*

Searching for sea glass. Digging for clams. Climbing a lighthouse. Battling sunburn and black flies. Surf–fishing at sunrise. Kayaking through foggy bogs. Shaking sand from your shoes. The memories made on the beaches of Cape Cod are as endless as the waves lapping at its shores. Any one who has spent glorious summer days baking in the sun and reveling in the evening breezes, understands how every grain of sand and strand of dune grass is precious to these experiences—and to the memories yet to be made.

Beginning in the 1850s, the Cape Cod Railroad carried the first tourists onto the Cape and one hundred years later, they continued coming by automobile. The steady growth of tourism in the early 1900s helped the Cape to recover from the decline in the fishing industry, but also led to the realization that its natural resources need to be protected.

The National Parks System surveyed the state of the historic and scenic infrastructure of the Outer Cape, from Chatham to Provincetown, and proposed the creation of a National Park. It encompassed a majority of the Outer Caper, which included commercial and residential properties. Some generations–old families were not happy about this, but in an unprecedented act, Congress crafted a bill using eminent domain and government money to secure private lands for a government–owned public park.

It took a few years and lots of creative negotiation before the bill was unanimously passed.

Senator John F. Kennedy recognized the need to preserve the Cape's natural beauty after having spent a lifetime summering on Cape Cod. He was one of the earliest supporters of the bill. On August 7, 1961, seven months after becoming President, Kennedy signed legislation to create the Cape Cod National Seashore. 44,000 acres of beachfront, dunes, bogs, marshland, ponds, trails, historic sites, and American heritage was placed in the care of the National Parks Service (*www.nps.gov/caco*) with which it remains.

Today, nearly four million visitors make an annual pilgrimage across the Cape Cod Canal and almost all of us, at some point, find our way to the Lower and Outer Cape. The Cape Cod National Seashore has, in a way, become Massachusetts' Disney World. It brings bundles of tourism money to the region, yet the human impact takes a toll on every aspect, from the beaches and dunes to the trails and wildlife. It is an expensive upkeep. The National Seashore was created as an effort to "freeze" things the way they were at that moment in time, which was impossible. The Cape remains at the mercy of tourists and Mother Nature. It is as much the travelers' responsibility as it is the government's to ensure that future generations are able to experience the splendor of the Cape's natural resources and ensure they take away the same sort of memories.

EXPERIENCE

Pick up a copy of writer and naturalist Henry Beston's 1928 book, *The Outermost House* and find a place along Coast Guard Beach to dig in. Wander along towering dunes of sand, taking in nature's sights, sounds, rhythms, and the magic that Beston's book so poetically captures. His sympathetic observations and reflections on Cape Cod life, combined with a Thoreauvian zeal for the natural environment contributed to the creation of the Cape Cod National Seashore some 30 years later. His concerns about preserving the local habitat remain relevant to this day. They served as the inspiration for the government claiming lands stretching from the barrier islands of Monomoy in Chatham to the dunes of the Province Lands in Provincetown.

The cottage where Beston lived and wrote once stood on the Outer Beach near the inlet to Nauset Marsh, but sadly, was swept away in the Great Storm of 1978. A nostalgic two–mile walk around this area is a wonderful way to experience the beauty of the "backside of Cape Cod"—a side that possessed such splendor that when faced with leaving the Cape, Beston "could not go."

The Cape Cod Chamber shares a list of organizations dedicated to preserving the unique natural and environmental habitat of the Cape(*www.capecodchamber.org/the_natural_environment*). Many of these organizations offer specialized seminars, guided tours, and educational events to bring awareness to those of us who appreciate the Cape's pristine beauty and want to help maintain it in the face of tourism.

The non–profit Association to Preserve Cape Cod (*www.apcc.org*) is the guardian of natural land resources such as dunes, meadows, marshes, and ponds. Another keeper of Cape Cod's National Seashore fauna is the Wellfleet Bay Wildlife Sanctuary. This division of the Massachusetts Audubon focuses on protecting threatened shorebirds, sea turtles, and crabs. Visit *www.massaudubon.org* to see the extensive trail system running through the Cape's forests, marshes and beachfront. A visit to the Esther Underwood Johnson Nature Center within the sanctuary, combined with a hike along any one of the numerous trails is a great way to experience the diversity of Cape Cod's National Seashore. It helps to understand exactly why this region is protected as a National Park. The sanctuary entrance is just over the Wellfleet/ Eastham town line near the Wellfleet Drive–in Theater.

Nearly 40 miles of Atlantic–facing coastline falls within the protected park zone and six swimming beaches are located within the National Seashore: Coast Guard Beach and Nauset Light Beach in Eastham, Marconi Beach in Wellfleet, Head of the Meadow Beach in Truro, and Race Point and Herring Cove in Provincetown. Daily car, bike, and pedestrian beach fees are charged from Memorial Day through September, but an annual Cape Cod National Seashore pass can be purchased for a reasonable price at parking–booths, the Salt Pond Visitor Center (Route 6, Eastham) and Province Lands Visitor Center (Race Point Road, Provincetown). These fees help to maintain public access to the beaches, parking lots, lifeguards, and bathrooms.

26
GHOST SHIP RISING

PROVINCETOWN
– 1985 –

One of the worst storms ever to hit Cape Cod sunk the infamous pirate "Black Sam" Bellamy's ship into the dark, tempestuous Atlantic Ocean on April 16, 1717. The violent wreck sent 144 of 146 crewmen aboard the *Whydah* to watery graves—just a mere 500 feet from the shores of Wellfleet. Romantic tales of Black Sam trying to reach his sweetheart, Maria Hallett, with a shipload of gold and silver plundered from European vessels in the Caribbean were passed down through the centuries. Plenty of attempts were made to locate the loot, but nothing more than a handful of gold coins turned up. Plus, there was no certainty these bits and baubles actually came from the *Whydah*. As time passed, few believed the stories were true and even fewer believed in the existence of this sunken treasure. Luckily, that few included a very passionate, persistent Barry Clifford.

A childhood filled with tales of pirates, combined with research and a relentless belief in the existence of the treasure, along with a little nudging from Walter Cronkite, turned Clifford into an underwater explorer. His boyhood dream of finding the treasure was still a long shot. First, the coastline along the outer Cape Cod has one of the highest concentrations of shipwrecks anywhere on the East Coast and the *Whydah*'s exact resting place was never confirmed. Second, there was a general disdain among academic archaeologists toward private archaeological adventures. After a lot of arm–twisting, legal wrangling, and penny–pinching, Team Whydah got underway in the early months of 1983.

Clifford pulled together a crew consisting of friends, fisherman, and fellow salvage divers after rallying private investors. Even John F. Kennedy Junior came along that first summer. The boat, appropriately named *Vast Explorer*, was modified for underwater exploration. Its maiden voyage was made from a boatyard in Maine down the coast to Wellfleet where it began a new life as a research vessel. The expedition muddled through the first season to no avail; the treasure hunters had nothing to show for all of their hard work.

The next few years beginning July 20, 1984, proved to be very different. Out of the sands of the Atlantic Ocean came cannons, gold bars, and hoards of gold and silver ingots and coins—and the swag just kept coming. The typical haul yielded artifact upon artifact: spoons, kettles, games, medical instruments, and weaponry. More than 6,000 gold coins and bars were recovered and placed in a vault, while thousand of other items were conserved or placed in storage

Items of a personal nature, such as buttons, clothing, jewelry, and even human bones, brought a sense of humanity to the long–gone crew. These artifacts helped to piece together what eighteenth–century life aboard a pirate ship looked like. It became abundantly clear that these lives were lost in a violent manner during a horrific storm. It also changed the traditional perception of the pirate world.

Clifford was certain he had discovered Blacks Sam's ship. It was in the correct location—no other wrecks in the area were documented as carrying such a trea- sure and there was no record of the booty having ever been recovered. Although Clifford and his crew uncovered nearly 20,000 objects, the Massachusetts Board of Underwater Archaeological Resources refused to recognize the finds as specifically from the *Whydah*.

The team knew exactly what it would take—a smoking gun. They had to discover something marked with the name of the ship, so there would be no doubt. The ships quarter board or the bell would do the trick, but did either still exist? The 1985 season was coming to a close. Winter would settle into Cape Cod very soon and money was in short supply. Little did the team know that within a few weeks, everything would change.

In early October, a large mass showed up on the magnetometer (an instrument used to find magnetic objects.) Divers noticed what appeared to be a bell–shaped object located close to the group of cannons discovered earlier in the season. Clifford dove down to have a look without getting his hopes up. Sure enough, it was a bell, but after 250 years under the salty sea, it was concreted—encrusted with layers of salt, silt, sand, and an illegible inscription.

It was impossible at that point to know to which ship the bell belonged, so emotions were kept in check. With the sheer volume of wrecks in the area, the bell could have come from any number of ships. The logical assumption was that the heaviest items, such as cannons and bells, sink quickly never too far from where the ship goes down.

On October 7, 1985, the unidentified bell was hoisted from the water and taken to a lab where it was submerged in a tank of fresh water with a mild electric current. In time, the current broke down the salts, and the lump of the concrete began crumbling away, exposing the word *gally*. This was certainly a different spelling of the modern word galley, which was a lightweight ship with a big cargo space — a favorite among Pirates, but there was still no recognizable name. Conservators patiently picked away at the rest of the concrete by hand. A big chunk fell away after 20 minutes revealing the name of the ship: "*Whydah Gally, 1716*".

Smoking gun, indeed! From that moment on, there was no question as to what Barry Clifford and his team of explorers had found: Black Sam Bellamy's legendary ship, *Whydah*, along with the Pirate Prince's sunken treasure. This is just the beginning of the story.

The *Whydah* became the first authenticated pirate ship discovered in North America and one of only two from which loot has been recovered. The treasure's value is rumored to be worth between $20 and $40 million, but the speculation spirals upward into the hundreds of millions. This small, privately–funded venture became an instant corporation—with bureaucracy, lawsuits, and all.

The expedition and conservation is still going on to this day. Among the 200,000 artifacts recovered are extraordinary objects, such as the world's oldest, reliably dated collection of Akan (West African) gold jewelry and the infamous bell. In 1998, the elusive remains of the ship's hull were found. The remarkable story of a legendary pirate and the man who brought him back to life is told through tantalizing exhibitions in the privately funded Whydah Museum in Provincetown.

EXPERIENCE

You'll find no proverbial rum bottles or eye–patches at the Whydah Museum (*www.whydah.com*), located at the end of Macmillan Pier in Provincetown. Just look for the sign with the skull and crossbones. The small museum is chock full of arti-facts, ranging from intimate personal items and clothing to navigational equipment and weapons. Among the must–sees is an important collection of West African gold jewelry, reinforcing the pirate's connection with the slave trade. The museum serves as a working lab, where the finds are exhibited while being cleaned, leaving a little to the imagination. The educational displays offer valuable and unexpected insight to eighteenth–century piracy.

Make like a pirate and head out to the open waters on a whale–watching excur-sion, departing from the wharf near the museum. Dolphin Fleet Whale Watch (*www.whalewatch.com*) offers daily boat tours to the Stellwagen Bank National Marine Sanctuary. Scan the water for whale's tails as the boat crew entertains with lively stories and ecological information. The boat trips sail along the Cape Cod National Seashore, offering the same views Black Sam had of the coastline. You might also encounter other local wildlife and cruise by lighthouses, which did not exist in the early eighteenth century. In good pirate form, grab a rum drink and sandwich from the bar and keep your camera handy for whale of an encounter.

Landlubbers might skip the boat ride and head to one of Provincetown's most iconic eateries: The Lobster Pot (321 Commercial Street /*www.ptownlobsterpot.com*). It is located just around the corner from the wharf. Grab a table overlooking the historic harbor and enjoy the gamut of fresh seafood, Portuguese specialties, and Tim's award–winning clam chowder. For an eagles' eye view of the water (and a stellar Bloody Mary), grab a cocktail at the restaurant's rooftop bar, Top of The Pot.

27

LIGHTING THE WAY: HIGHLAND LIGHT

TRURO
– 1996 –

For eighteen days in June 1996, a piece of history was not being made, but being moved. The 404–ton Highland Light, now known as the Cape Cod Light, was meticulously raised from its foundations and slowly rolled to a new position away from the eroding cliff. Today, Cape Cod's first and tallest lighthouse continues to aid sailors navigating the treacherous coast and serves as a historical beacon for tourists, photographers, artists, and history buffs.

This section of Cape Cod has earned the menacing nickname, "Graveyard of the Atlantic" for the thousand documented ships that have sunk between Truro and Wellfleet. The worst of it, however, lies about a mile northeast of present–day Truro, near the bend in the "wrist" of the Cape. Congress was petitioned for a lighthouse as far back as 1794 because the shifting sands of Peaked Hill Bar were considered one of the most perilous stretches of coast in the country. More ships are wrecked off Truro's eastern shore than in any other part of Cape Cod according to the Boston Marine Society.

A lighthouse was of dire necessity in this region and there was no better place for it than the highlands of North Truro. Towering cliffs and sand dunes reminiscent of Scotland's coast plunge 125–feet into Atlantic Ocean. The hillside is comprised of compacted clay deposits that the lighthouse engineers believed would withstand the hammering of waves. This plea struck a chord with Congress.

In 1797, President George Washington commissioned Cape Cod's first lighthouse to be built—the twentieth in the United States. The following year, ten strategic acres of land were purchased from Isaac Small of Truro. A forty–five–foot tall, wooden lighthouse was constructed 500 feet from the edge of the bluff. Small was appointed the keeper of Cape Cod's first lighthouse, appropriately dubbed the Highland Light.

Its powerful lantern, which sat 160 feet above sea level, contained 24 lamps and reflectors fueled by whale oil. Fearing this light might be confused with the Boston Light, a rotating eclipser was installed to make it appear to flash when viewed from a ship. Although it was on a very slow, eight–minute rotation, the Highland Light was our country's first lighthouse to utilize a "flashing" light.

Just a few years later, both the eclipser and the lighthouse keeper were replaced. In 1811, the lantern was updated with a more efficient Winslow Lewis reflector–lamp–based system, which required a little more work than Keeper Small was willing to do. After complaining about the newfangled lamps, he was ousted for a more willing seventy–year old who would last only five years.

By 1828, the thirty–year–old lighthouse had taken a beating by Mother Nature and was in "very imperfect" condition. Winds frequently rattled the structure, repeatedly breaking the glass lanterns. The lighthouse was rebuilt in brick after being deemed unsafe in 1831. Shortly afterward, a new lantern, staircase, and windows were installed, but according to then lighthouse keeper, Jesse Holbrook, the tower had been hastily constructed without regard to proper mortar and bond.

No matter how poorly constructed the new, brick structure might have been, the lighthouse served its purpose better than the original wooden one. The keepers made do until 1857, at which time the importance of this light could not be ignored. Ship after ship continued to be lost in the treacherous waters near Truro, prompting yet another face–lift to the tower and the replacement of the reflector system with a new, high–tech Fresnel lens, direct from Paris. Highland Light was now one of the East Coast's most powerful and vital lighthouses. Henry David Thoreau visited in the 1850s, declaring the light in "apple pie order" and went on to write a history of the lighthouse for *Atlantic Monthly* in 1864.

The issuance of a coal–burning fog signal, powerful enough to cut through the shore's regular murky haze, attested even more so to the importance of this station. The keeper was also given two assistants and his house was reinforced in brick. At the turn of the century, Highland Light was often, quite literally, the first glimpse of America seen by European immigrants. In 1904, an important naval radio station was installed on-site, and during World War I, Marines guarded the strategically located lighthouse.

The Highland Light was electrified in 1932, making its four million footcandle lantern the most powerful on the coast. It was visible in stormy weather from as far as 45 miles out and could be seen as far as 75 miles away when the weather was clear. Highland Light was automated in 1986, but the house remained in use as Coast Guard lodging rather than as a light keeper's dwelling.

The lighthouse stood only 500 feet from the cliff's edge when it was built in 1797. Henry David Thoreau documented the loss of forty feet in one year alone in 1856 and another forty feet slipped away in a winter gale in 1990. By the mid–1990s, the steep clay bluffs, which two hundred years earlier were substantial enough to carry the heavy lighthouse load, had experienced such significant erosion that the building was only a hundred feet away from toppling into the Atlantic. Today, less than four of the original ten acres that were purchased from Small still exist. Highland Light, which was in the business of saving lives, now needed rescuing of its own.

The Truro Historical Society undertook the monumental task of moving the Highland Light to a safer position. Its "Save the Light" committee raised more than $150,000. This combined with $1.5 million in federal and state funds paid for the move of the light and the keeper's house. In June 1996, the three–week project began.

During the first several days, the foundation of the tower was excavated and four levels of beams were inserted under the lighthouse in a criss–cross fashion. Hydraulic jacks then lifted the entire structure onto rollers, which were then set on rails. Thousands of onlookers watched as the sixty–six–foot lighthouse inched its way inland. Coins, which were laid on the rails and flattened as the lighthouse rolled over them, were subsequently auctioned off with the proceeds going to the Truro Historical Society.

During the move of Highland Light there were a few hiccups, but eighteen days later it successfully arrived at its new home 450 feet away from the eroding cliff. It currently stands near the seventh fairway of the Highland Links golf course, where the worst danger is no longer Mother Nature, but errant golf balls.

The Highland Light was inaugurated in its new locale on Sunday, November 3, 1996, with guided tours, a relighting ceremony, and the Highland Light Bagpipe Band performing in full regalia. It is currently the country's fourth most powerful lighthouse. The light itself remains in the care of the United States Coast Guard while partners of the National Park Service operate the museum. Its official name was changed to Cape Cod Light in 1976. Modern day maritime charts refer to it as such, but to most Cape Codders it will forever be Highland Light.

EXPERIENCE

Drive along Route 6 and exit at Highland Road, South Highland Road or South Hollow Roads, each of which leads to Highland Light Road. A short way down the road, the lighthouse stands amidst a links–style golf course, well away from the windswept, eroding bluffs. Take a guided tour of the Highland House Museum (10 Highland Light Road/ *www.highlandlighthouse.org*) and climb 69 steps up the narrow, circular staircase for stunning vistas over the Atlantic Ocean and Cape Cod Bay. On a clear day, visibility reaches up to twenty miles.

Make an afternoon of it by staying to play nine holes at Cape Cod's oldest golf course. Highland Links (*www.highlandlinkscapecod.com*), built in 1892, runs along the scenic cliffs, inland through moors, and around the lighthouse. In true Scottish–links form, this course incorporates a deep rough, non–irrigated open fairways, and lots of woody Scotch Broom and heath. Afterwards, stop for a wine tasting and tour of Truro Vineyards (Route 6A, North Truro / *www.trurovineyardsofcapecod.com*), situated on Route 6A just past the Route 6 and 6A split. You can't miss the 2,100 gallon wine barrel perched on the tower. Get schooled in the art of maritime grape growing while sipping on lovely Chardonnay, Merlot or Cabernet Franc in the cozy tasting room of the 1830s farmhouse. The Triumph Meritage red blend is bold and distinct, just like the Truro landscape.

For a completely different perspective on the drama that Mother Nature imparts upon the Truro coast, follow the road down to the most beautiful beach at Long Nook in Truro. From the eroding cliffs above to the towering dunes below, you'll see how Mother Nature giveth and taketh away. Climb down the sandy path, then look up at the dramatic landscape for a truly humbling experience. The magnificence of the surroundings is even more evocative when the weather is moody. Parking at Long Nook is limited and in season, a parking permit is required.

28
CAPE COD TRIVIA

DID YOU KNOW?

Historians theorize that Icelandic Vikings might have been the first visitors to Cape Cod around A.D. 1004. The 13th-century Norse Saga titled, *Flateyjarbok* (Flat Island Book) gives vivid descriptions of Leif Ericson's journeys across the Atlantic to an area he named "vinland." Some historians believe this to be along the Cape Cod coast but they lack archaeological evidence.

The first recorded European shipwreck off America's east coast happened December 12, 1626. The pilgrim's small boat, *Sparrowhawk,* was grounded in a storm off Nauset Beach. The skeletal wooden remains of the ship are on display in the Cape Cod Maritime Museum in Hyannis.

April 1717, the *Whydah* pirate ship sunk off the coast of South Wellfleet in a brutal storm. The slave–ship taken by "Black Sam" Bellamy was named for the port city of Ouidah in today's west African country of Benin. More than 400 pieces of West African Akan gold jewelery were recovered in the wreckage. These important finds offer insight into the culture and arts of the eighteenth century Slave and Gold Coasts

One of the oldest structures on Cape Cod is the Judah Baker Windmill, constructed in 1791. The Mill began life in South Dennis and was subsequently moved to Kelley's Pond in Dennis before landing in its current resting place on River Street in South Yarmouth in 1866.

Nantucket resident and amateur astronomer, Maria Mitchell made the first documented sighting of a comet in 1847. This discovery led to her becoming the first woman elected to the American Academy of Arts and Sciences and the first admitted to the Association for the Advancement of Science.

Author, Thornton Waldo Burgess was born in Sandwich on January 14, 1874. This naturalist, conservationist, and prolific story–teller drew inspiration from his Cape Cod surroundings to create the beloved characters of his *Peter Rabbit* stories. The Green Briar Nature Center & Jam Kitchen, adjacent to the famed brier patch, offers Peter Rabbit programs for kids, plus gardening, preserves, and jam workshops for adults. It is operated by the Thornton W. Burgess Society (*www.thorntonburgess.org*) at 6 Discovery Hill Road off of Route 6A in East Sandwich.

Learn about crime and punishment at America's oldest wooden jail, located at 3353 Main Street (Old King's Highway) in the village of Barnstable. The Old Gaol was built on the order of the Plymouth and Massachusetts Bay Colony. It served as a jail from 1620 until 1820 when the county realized space was required for more than six prisoners. The jail was moved to its present location on the grounds of the Coast Guard Heritage Museum and was awarded Historic Landmark status in the early 1970s.

Wellfleet sea dog, Lorenzo Dow Baker, was the first to import bananas to the United States and established the United Fruit Company (now, Chiquita Brands International) in 1881.

In 1899, Charles Hawthorne established the Cape Cod School of Art in Provincetown, American's first school dedicated solely to Impressionist painting. The Provincetown Art Colony (also established by Hawthorne) has been the refuge of artists since 1914, making P'town the longest continuously running art colony in the country.

Henry Beston's famous book, *The Outermost House,* published in 1928, gives a nostalgic account of the year this naturalist lived in a cottage on the Great Dune of Eastham. His writings helped to bring about the creation of the Cape Cod National Seashore and influenced subsequent generations of ecologists, biologists and conservationists.

Wellfleet resident, Luther Crowell invented the square–bottom paper bag in 1872.

Harry Hibbard Kemp (1883–1960), the actor and "Tramp Poet" from Youngstown, Ohio, was a prolific writer who lived out his later life in a shanty on the Provincetown dunes. Kemp was famously nicknamed "The Poet of the Dunes" and notorious for seducing the wives of a few other famous writers, including Upton Sinclair.

President Grover Cleveland summered in Bourne at his residence named Gray Gables, which burned down in the 1970s. He was the first to establish a summer White House on Cape Cod.

The clock in the steeple of Wellfleet's First Congregational Church keeps ship's time or Greenwich Mean Time (GMT).

The Woods Hole Oceanographic Institution (WHOI), founded in 1930, is a research facility dedicated to all aspects of marine science. It is located on the point just south of the town of Falmouth and is the largest independent oceanographic institute in the world.

On July 25, 1956, two ocean liners traveling at full speed through thick fog collided off the island of Nantucket. The luxury Italian liner *Andrea Doria* with 1700 souls on board was struck in the side by the Swedish ship, *Stockholm*. Both ships sunk in 225 feet of icy water, taking 51 lives with them.

The Kennedy family sweated out the 1960 election at their compound in Hyannisport. John F. Kennedy gave a short speech at the National Guard Armory in Hyannis after being elected the 35th president of the United States. The Kennedy family put Cape Cod in the international spotlight for years to come.

The Wampanoag Tribe of Gay Head (Aquinnah) on Martha's Vineyard became a federally acknowledged tribe through an act of Congress in 1987. Its Tribal Lands include Gay Head Cliffs, Herring Creek, Lobsterville, and parts of Christiantown and Chappaquiddick.

In 1945, a young African American woman, Eugenia Fortes was told by the police to leave the then segregated East Beach in Hyannisport. This refusal launched her civil rights activism and founding of the Cape Cod chapter of the NAACP in 1961. On August 28, 2004, East Beach was renamed Fortes Beach in her honor.

Eight working lights on the Cape make it, mile–for–mile, one of the world's largest concentrations of lighthouses.

The village of Dennis boasts America's oldest working pipe organ, located in the Congregational Church of South Dennis on Main Street.

The Cape Playhouse, a former 19th century Unitarian Meeting House also in Dennis is the longest running summer theater in America.

The Methodist Tabernacle, built in 1879, is one of the country's largest wrought iron framed buildings. The pavilion stands in the heart of Oak Bluffs on Martha's Vineyard. It once served as the site of regular Methodist camp meetings, but now hosts summer events, music and church services. The 130–foot wide, open air pavilion seats 3,000 and stands in the middle of Trinity Park surrounded by colorful Victorian 'gingerbread" cottages.

The Dune Shacks of Peaked Hill Bars is a national landmarked historic district in Provincetown and Truro named for the Peaked Hill Bars Life–Saving Station established in 1882. The primitive dune shacks drew American artists and writers from the 1920s through today, the most famous including Jack Kerouac, Jackson Pollock, Eugene O'Neill, and self–proclaimed "poet of the dunes," Harry Kemp.

The contradictory–seeming terms "Lower Cape" (northern region) and "Upper Cape" (southern region) originated as sailors sailing from the south to the north would have had southerly winds to their backs, therefore sailing "down–wind" to the Lower Cape.

Eight Strawberry Lane in Yarmouth Port sounds like a sweet little slice of heaven, but this is the house where Edward Gorey lived. The interesting little home–turned–museum is a shrine to the extraordinary illustrator, author, and playwright. Gorey (1925–2000) is most famous for his macabre alphabet book, *The Gashlycrumb Tinies*, and other dark, unsettling musings. He lived in this former sea captain's home since 1979. As an avid animal–lover, his trust supports animal rescue and welfare organizations. The eclectic Edward Gorey House is a must for cat and cartoon lovers alike.

29

DISCOVERING CAPE COD

This travel compendium provides reliable suggestions on where to eat, drink, and have a cultural experience. An effort is made to include a cross-section of eateries popular with tourists, locals, families, and couples, which include both high-end and reasonably priced places. Food defines a culture, region or city, so this section nods heavily toward restaurants and markets. Explorers gotta eat, right?

Keep in mind the peak season travel pointers included here, especially as related to beach parking and generally getting around between Memorial Day and Labor Day. A great time to visit is the fall, just after Labor Day when the water is at its warmest and crowds have thinned. Chances are you will have glorious, sunny beach days with chilly autumn evenings. No matter what time of year you visit, the landscape is evocative. and it will not take long to recognize the deep history, culture, and heritage that permeates every nook and cranny of Cape Cod.

TRAVELING THE CAPE

As the temperature rise during peak season, so do the prices, crowds, traffic, parking restrictions, and restaurant waits. When visiting in the summer, it is best to come armed with patience.

Accessing the Cape is straightforward, with only two roads leading on and off of the Cape and one major highway thoroughfare. Getting to where you need to be during the summer season can be a slow process, especially on Friday and Sunday afternoons when the weekend crowds arrive and depart en masse. Once again, patience and a good map are invaluable.

Crossing over the Cape Cod Canal is a breathtaking experience as the road arches up over the man–made passage linking Cape Cod Bay with Buzzard's Bay. Arriving via the Sagamore Bridge lands you on Route 6, also known as the Mid–Cape

Highway, which runs all the way to Provincetown. Cross at the Bourne Bridge if your destination is south on Route 28 toward Falmouth or Cotuit.

Navigating the Cape is easy. Cape Cod's three main roads originate at the Sagamore and Bourne Bridges, splitting into north, south, and central thoroughfares. U.S. Route 6 is the larger highway, while the commercialized Route 28 dips south then east and follows along the south coast of the Cape. Route 6A, the scenic Old Kings Highway, runs east then north along the bay, splitting off at Truro for a picturesque waterfront drive into Provincetown.

The main artery, Route 6, stretches about 70 miles along the center of Cape Cod all the way out to the "sandy fist" at P-town. A four-lane freeway with exits for each of the major towns comprises the first 50 miles. It then narrows to two lanes upon reaching the rotary at Eastham in the Outer Cape.

Routes 28 and 6A are slower moving with only two lanes and many more stoplights. Taking these slow roads, especially in shoulder or off-season, is always a more preferable option if you have time to savor the journey. Route 28 is lined with shopping centers, malls, and seemingly endless motels and putt-putt courses, until it reaches the picturesque towns and harbors around Dennis Port, Harwich Port, and South Chatham. Route 6A makes for an entirely beautiful, scenic drive through the heart of many charming Cape Cod villages, over foggy bogs, and along sandy dunes.

Allow for extra travel time during the summer, especially on the slower roads. 25-mile back-ups are not uncommon in the event of an accident, holiday, or during the regular weekend crush. Getting around the Cape in off-season is more or less a breeze outside of the normal business rush hour.

Beach parking lots charge a daily fee from Memorial Day to Labor Day. If staying for a week or longer, a parking sticker is the easiest and most affordable way to go beach hopping. Permits can be purchased at the visitor's centers in bigger towns, such as Hyannis, Orleans, and Provincetown. In some cases, the smallest beaches require remote parking and shuttling to the waterfront, which may not be ideal for families hauling a carload of kids and gear. For a full list of beach regulations go to *www.oncape.com/beaches*. These same beach lots are free in the fall and winter, between Labor Day and Memorial Day. Just check the signage, as many parking lots do not charge after 3 or 4 PM during peak travel season. When it comes to Cape Cod beaches, reading the signs and using common sense is the best approach.

An alternative to battling the roads and parking lots is to leave your car behind and go exploring on two wheels (or by foot). At the easier end of the biking difficulty scale, is the Cape Cod Canal as suggested in the Experience for *Bourne Free Enterprise*. Looking for a more rigorous ride? Peddle the hilly Province Land Dunes just outside of Provincetown, where beautiful scenery and a good workout is guaranteed.

The Rails to Trails system takes advantage of the defunct railroad lines that once carried tourists from the mainland onto the Cape. The Cape Cod Rail Trail now runs a mostly unbroken 22 miles from Dennis to Wellfleet, through Harwich, Brewster, Orleans, and Eastham. The paved paths are wide enough in many areas to accommodate cyclists, runners, and horseback riders. Busy road crossings are well marked, as are the opportunities to digress onto side trails leading to beaches, forests and ponds. Bike rentals are common all over the Cape, but call Nickerson State Park (508–896–3491) for details on rental options along the Rail Trail.

The next few pages include suggestions for places to eat, drink, and experience a cultural side to the Cape. This section is organized by region: Upper/Mid, Lower/Mid, Outer, Martha's Vineyard, and Nantucket.

UPPER CAPE

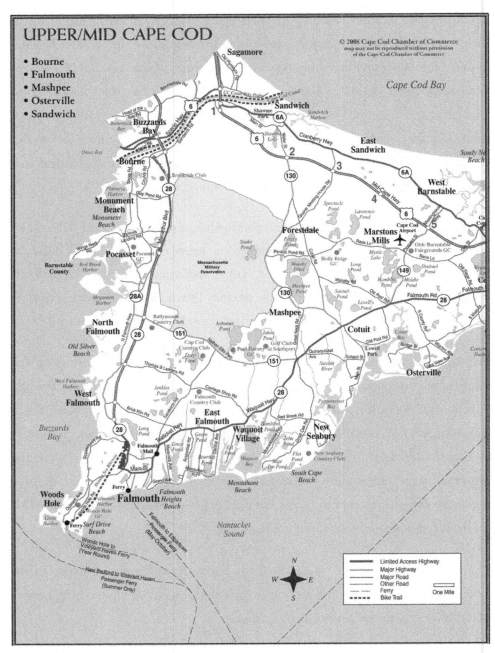

DINING

Beehive Tavern, 406 Route 6A, East Sandwich / *www.thebeehivetavern.com*

Belfry Inn and Bistro, 6 Jarves Street, Sandwich / *www.belfryinn.com*

British Beer Company, 263 Grand Avenue, Falmouth / *www.britishbeer.com*

The Brown Jug, 155 Main Street, Sandwich / *www.thebrownjug.com*

Dan'l Webster Inn, 149 Main Street, Sandwich / *www.danlwebsterinn.com*

Five Bays Bistro, 825 Main Street, Osterville / *www.fivebaysbistro.com*

Glass Onion, 37 North Main Street, Falmouth / *www.theglassoniondining.com*

La Cucina Sul Mare, 237 Main Street, Falmouth / *www.lacucinasulmare.com*

Osteria La Civetta, 143 Main Street, Falmouth / *www.osterialacivetta.com*

Trevi Café, Mashpee Commons, 25 Market Street, Mashpee / *www.trevicafe.com*

FARMERS' MARKETS

Tuesday: Sandwich Farmers' Market and Green Harvest Farmers' Market in East Falmouth / Wednesday: Market at Oak Crest in Sandwich/ Thursday: Falmouth Farmers' Market / Saturday: Mashpee Commons Farmers' Market

MUSEUMS

Cape Cod Children's Museum, Mashpee

Coast Guard Heritage Museum, Barnstable

Heritage Museum and Garden, Sandwich

Sandwich Glass Museum, Sandwich

Wampanoag Indian Museum, Mashpee

FESTIVALS

Mashpee Wampanoag Powwow (July) *www.mashpeewampanoagtribe.com/powwow*

Celebrate the past and present culture of Cape Cod's indigenous Americans at the fairgrounds in East Falmouth every July. Pick up Native American handicrafts and food. Traditional dancers, singers, and drummers perform, and other spiritual activities take place during the weekend.

Scallop Fest (September) *www.scallopfest.org*

East Falmouth has been paying homage to the meaty mollusk every September for more than a half century. The three–day celebration showcases the scallop in every form, both at the fair and in local restaurants.

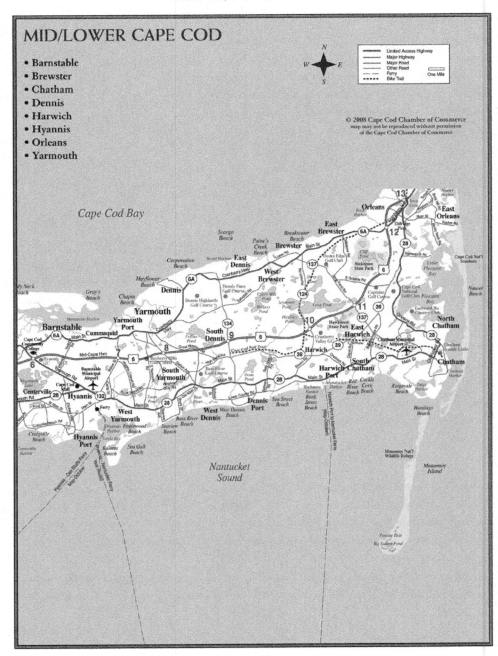

MID-CAPE

DINING

Alberto's Ristorante, 360 Main Street, Hyannis / *www.albertos.net*
Ann and Fran's, 471 Route 28, West Yarmouth
Baxter's Boathouse, 177 Pleasant Street, Hyannisport / *www.Baxterscapecod.com*
Brazilian Grille Churrascaria, 680 Main Street, Hyannis / *www.braziliangrill-capecod.com*
Fin Seafood, 800 Main Street, Dennis / *www.fincapecod.com*
Grumpy's, 1408 Route 6A, East Dennis / *www.grumpyscapecod.com*
Inaho, 157 Route 6A, Yarmouth Port / *www.inahocapecod.com*
The Keltic Kitchen, 415 Route 28, West Yarmouth / *www.keltickitchen.com*
Lamb and Lion Inn, 2504 Main Street, Barnstable / *www.lambandlion.com*
Naked Oyster, 410 Main Street, Hyannis / *www.nakedoyster.com*
The Ocean House, 425 Old Wharf Road, Dennisport / *www.oceanhouserestaurant.com*
Old Yarmouth Inn, 223 Route 6A, Yarmouth Port / *www.oldyarmouthinn.com*
Pan d'Avignon, 15 Hinckley Road, Hyannis / *www.pandavignon.com*
Red Cottage, 36 Old Bass River Road, South Dennis / *www.redcottagerestaurant.com*
Red Pheasant Inn, 905 Main Street, Dennis / *www.redpheasantinn.com*
Skipper Restaurant, 152 South Shore Drive, South Yarmouth / *www.skipperrestaurant.com*
Sundancers, 116 Main Street, West Dennis / *www.sundancerscapecod.com*
Twenty Eight Atlantic, Waquassett Inn, 2173 Route 28, Harwich Port / *www.wequassett.com*
Ocean House, 425 Old Wharf Road, Dennis Port / *www.oceanhouserestaurant.com*

FARMERS' MARKETS

Wednesday: Mid-Cape Farmers' Marketing Hyannis / Thursday: Bass River Farmers' Market, Yarmouth / Friday: Osterville Farmers' Market / Saturday: Barnstable Farmers' Market & Dennis Farmers' Market

MUSEUMS

Cape Cod Baseball League Hall of Fame, Hyannis
Cape Cod Maritime Museum, Hyannis
Cape Cod Museum of Art, Dennis
Edward Gorey House, Yarmouth Port

John F. Kennedy Museum, Hyannis

FESTIVALS

Cape Cod Maritime Days (May) *www.capecodmaritimedays.com*
The month–long celebration of Cape Cod's rich maritime history is celebrated throughout the month of May with Cape–wide festivals and events.
Cape & Islands Orchid Show (January) *www.caios.org*
For more than a quarter century, the flower fans converge on Hyannis to celebrate the tropical tubers. The show includes plants displays, orchid art, garden suppliers and educational programs.
Yarmouth Seaside Festival (October) *www.yarmouthseasidefestival.com*
The three-day event held in South Yarmouth during Columbus Day weekend features food, music, a big craft fair, lots of contests, a 5K, and a kayak and canoe race.

LOWER–CAPE

DINING

Abba Restaurant, 89 Old Colony Way, Orleans / *www.abbarestaurant.com*
Brax Landing, 705 Route 28, Harwich / *www.braxlanding.com*
Brewster Fish House, 2208 Main Street, Brewster / *www.brewsterfishhouse.com*
Captain Cass, 117 Rock Harbor Road, Orleans
Chatham Bars Inn, 297 Shore Road, Chatham / *www.chathambarsinn.com*
Chillingsworth, 2449 Main Street, Brewster / w*ww.chillingsworth.com*
Del Mar Bar and Bistro, 907 Main Street, Chatham / *www.delmarbistro.com*
Impudent Oyster, 15 Chatham Bars Avenue, Chatham
Mahoney Atlantic Bar & Grill, 28 Main Street, Orleans / *www.mahoneysatlantic.com*
Pisces Restaurant, 2653 Main Street, South Chatham / *www.piscesofchatham.com*
Ruggies, 707 Main Street, Harwich / *www.ruggiescapecod.com*
The Squire, 487 Main Street, Chatham / *www.thesquire.com*

FARMERS' MARKETS

Tuesday: Chatham Farmers' Market / Thursday: Harwich Farmers' Market / Saturday: Orleans Farmers' Market

MUSEUMS

Atwood House Museum, Chatham
Cape Cod Museum of Natural History, Brewster
Chatham Railroad Museum, Chatham

FESTIVALS

Annual Lighting of Pilgrim Monument. (November)
Thousands of lights illuminate the tower around Thanksgiving in celebration of the Pilgrims first landing.

Harwich's Cranberry, Arts and Music Festival (September) *www.harwichcranberryfestival.org*
Each autumn the flaming red fruits of Cape Cod's cranberry bogs are celebrated with a two day event just after Labor Day.

The ClamBQ (September) *www.clambq.com*
Orleans Food and music festival celebrates the end of summer with live music, local food and drink, craft fair, and a traditional clam bake and barbecue dinner.

OUTER CAPE

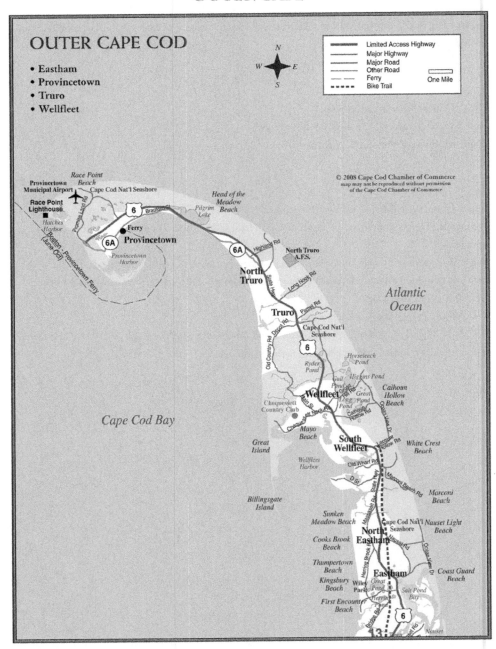

OUTER CAPE COD

- Eastham
- Provincetown
- Truro
- Wellfleet

N
W · E
S

| Limited Access Highway |
| Major Highway |
| Major Road |
| Other Road |
| Ferry | One Mile |
| Bike Trail |

© 2008 Cape Cod Chamber of Commerce
map may not be reproduced without permission
of the Cape Cod Chamber of Commerce

Race Point
Beach
Provincetown
Municipal Airport — Cape Cod Nat'l Seashore
Race Point
Lighthouse
Hatches
Harbor
Boston - Provincetown Ferry
(June-Oct)

Head of the
Meadow
Beach
Pilgrim
Lake

6
Bradford

Ferry
6A Provincetown

Provincetown
Harbor

6A Highland Rd

North Truro
A.F.S.

North
Truro

State Hwy

Long Nook Rd

Atlantic
Ocean

Truro
Pamet Rd

Dhon Rd

Old Country Rd

Cape Cod Nat'l
Seashore

6

Ryder
Pond

Horseleech
Pond

Gull
Pond

Higgins Pond

Wellfleet
Main St

Great
Pond

Long Pond

Calhoun
Hollow
Beach

Chequessett
Country Club

Mayo
Beach

Cannon Hill Rd

South
Wellfleet

White Crest
Beach

Cape Cod Bay

Great
Island

Wellfleet
Harbor

Old Wharf Rd

D St

Marconi Beach Rd

Marconi
Beach

Billingsgate
Island

Sunken
Meadow Beach

Cape Cod Nat'l
Seashore

Nauset Light
Beach

Cooks Brook
Beach

North
Eastham

Thumpertown
Beach

Ocean View Dr

Coast Guard
Beach

Kingsbury
Beach

Wiley
Park

Great
Pond

Eastham

First Encounter
Beach

Salt Pond
Bay

6

13

Nauset

DISCOVERING CAPE COD

DINING

Blackfish, 17 Truro Center Road, Truro

Laura & Tony's Kitchen, 5960 Route 6, Eastham / *www.lauraandtonyskitchen.com*

Lobster Pot, 321 Commercial Street, Provincetown / *www.ptownlobsterpot.com*

Local Break, 4450 State Highway, Eastham / *www.local-break.com*

Mac's Seafood, 264 Commercial Street, Wellfleet / *www.macsseafood.com*

The Mews Restaurant & Cafe, 429 Commercial Street, Provincetown / *www.mews.com*

PB Boulangerie, 17 LeCount Hollow Road, Wellfleet / *www.pbboulangeriebistro.com*

Portuguese Bakery, 299 Commercial Street, Provincetown

The Red Inn, 15 Commercial Street, Provincetown / *www.theredinn.com*

Truro Vineyards, 11 Shore Road, North Truro / *www.trurovineyardsofcapecod.com*

FARMER'S MARKETS

Monday: Truro Farmers' Market / Wednesday: Wellfleet Farmers' Market / Saturday: Provincetown Farmers' Market

MUSEUMS

Pilgrim Monument and Museum, Provincetown

Provincetown Art Association and Museum, Provincetown

Whydah Museum, Provincetown

FESTIVALS

Carnival (August) *www.ptown.org/carnival*

Early August brings an unleashing of fabulousness in Provincetown. After 35 years of parading Gay Pride through the streets, Carnival has grown to become one of Massachusetts's largest and Cape Cod's most popular outdoor festivals.

Eastham Windmill Weekend (September) *www.easthamchamber.com*

Celebrate the town of Eastham's heritage during this weekend festival centered around the historic windmill. The event includes sand art, live music and a classic car show.

Wellfleet Oyster Festival (October) *www.harwichcranberryfestival.org*

The two-day festival in mid-October celebrates the town's long history of shell-fishing, drawing upward of 25,000 people. The 'Fest a shucking good time full of food, art, music and games.

MARTHA'S VINEYARD

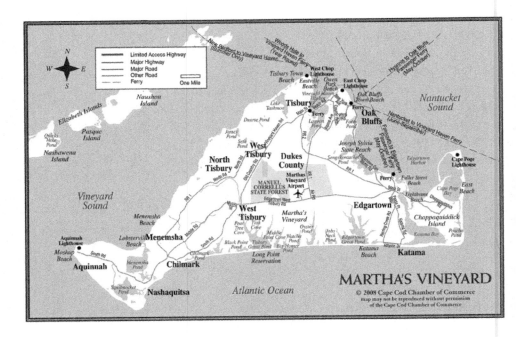

DINING

Among the Flowers Cafe, Mayhew Lane, Edgartown

Art Cliff Diner, 39 Beach Road, Vineyard Haven

Atria, 137 Main Street, Edgartown / *www.atriamv.com*

Black Dog Cafe, Vineyard Haven / *www.theblackdog.com*

The Copper Wok, 9 Main Street, Vineyard Haven / *www.copperwokmv.com*

Detente Restaurant, 15 Winter Street, Edgartown / *www.detentemv.com*

L'Etoile, 22 N. Water Street, Edgartown / *www.letoile.net*

Linda Jean's Restaurant, 25 Circuit Avenue, Oak Bluffs / *www.lindajeansrestaurant.com*

Little House Café, 339 State Road, Vineyard Haven / *www.littlehousemv.com*

Lucky Hank's Restaurant and Café, 218 Upper Main Street, Edgartown

Martha's Vineyard Chowder Company, 9 Oak Bluffs Avenue, Oak Bluffs / *www.mvchowder.com*

Offshore Ale Company , 30 Kennebec Avenue, Oak Bluffs / *www.offshoreale.com*

Red Cat Kitchen, 14 Kennebec Avenue, Oak Bluffs / *www.redcatkitchen.com*

Slice of Life, 50 Circuit Avenue, Oak Bluffs, MA / *www.sliceoflifemv.com*
The Sweet Life Café, 63 Circuit Avenue, Oak Bluffs / *www.sweetlifemv.com*
Waterside Market, 76 Main Street, Vineyard Haven / *www.watersidemarket.com*

MARKETS

20ByNine, 16 Kennebec Avenue, Oak Bluffs
Edgartown Meat and Fish Market, 138 Cooke Street, Edgartown
Fiddlehead Farm Market, 632 State Road, West Tisbury
Larson's Fish Market, 56 Basin Road, Chilmark
Menemsha Fish Market, 54 Basin Road, Chilmark
Morning Glory Farm, 120 Meshacket Road, Edgartown
Tisbury Farm Market, 342 State Road, Vineyard Haven
Vineyard Grocer, 294 State Road, Vineyard Haven

MUSEUMS

Aquinnah Cultural Center, Aquinnah
Cottage Museum, Oak Bluffs
Flying Horses Carousel, Oak Bluffs
Martha's Vineyard Museum, Edgartown
Old Sculpin Gallery, Edgartown
Vincent House Museum, Edgartown

FESTIVALS

Martha's Vineyard Agricultural Fair (August) *www.mvas.vineyard.net/new/annual-fair/*
The bounty of Martha's Vineyard has been celebrated in mid–August for more than 150 years. This is a real old–fashioned fête of all things local, with a livestock show and four–day fair sponsored by the MV Agricultural Society.

NANTUCKET

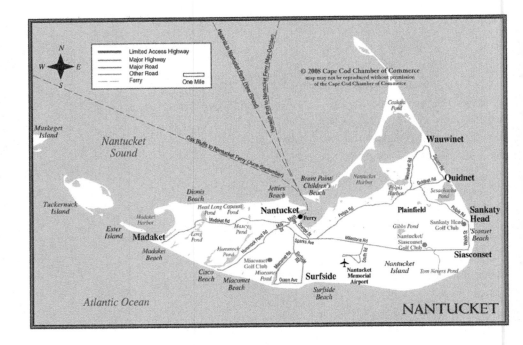

DINING

29 Fair, 29 Fair Street / 29fairack.com / *www.29fairstreetinn.com*

Centre Street Bistro, 29 Centre Street / *www.nantucketbistro.com*

Fog Island Cafe, 7 South Water Street / *www.fogisland.com*

Le Languedoc Inn & Bistro, 24 Broad Street / *www.languedocinn.com*

Petticoat Row Bakery, 35 Centre Street

White Elephant, 50 Easton Street / *www.whiteelephanthotel.com*

MARKETS

Farmers' Markets: Monday – Saturday: Bartlett's Farm Market (33 Barlett Farm Road / *www.barlettsfarm.com*) / Saturday: The Sustainable Nantucket Farmers & Artisans Market

Bartlett's Farm, 33 Bartlett Farm Road

Cowboy's Meat Market & Deli, 7 Bayberry Court

Sayle's Seafood, 99 Washington Street ext.

Sconset Market, 4 Main Street, Siasconset

MUSEUMS

Great Point Lighthouse

Loines Observatory

Maria Mitchell Aquarium

Maria Mitchell House, Natural Science Museum and Vestal Street Observatory

Museum of African American History, Nantucket

Nantucket Shipwreck and Lifesaving Museum, Nantucket

Nantucket Whaling Museum, Nantucket

Sankaty Head Lighthouse

FESTIVALS

Nantucket Book Festival (June) *www.nantucketbookfestival.org*

Literature lovers, rejoice! Local authors come together at various location around Nantucket. to speak and hold book signings. Special food, drink and museum events are also on the schedule throughout the weekend in mid-June.

Nantucket Wine Festival (May) *www.nantucketwinefestival.com*

Kick off summer on the island with a grand tasting of global wines, superb regional cuisine, and local music on the lawn of the elegant White Elephant Inn. The Wine Fest is usually held the weekend before Memorial Day.

BIBLIOGRAPHY & SOURCES

Anderson, Robert Charles. *The Great Migration Begins: Immigrants to new England 1620-1633*. 3 vols. Boston: New England Historic Genealogical Society, 1995.

Axtell, James. *The Invasion Within: The Contest of Cultures in Colonial North America* New York: Oxford University Press, 1985.

Barlow, Raymond E. and Joan E. Kaiser. *The Glass Industry in Sandwich, Vol. 1*. Atglen, PA.: Schiffer Publishing, Ltd., 1993.

Bradford, William. *Of Plymouth Plantation*. Edited by Samuel Eliot Morison. New York: Alfred A. Knopf, 1989.

Bragdon, Kathleen J. *Native People of Southern New England, 1500-1600*. Norman, OK: University of Oklahoma Press, 1996.

Champlain, Samuel de. *Voyages of Samuel de Champlain, 1604-1618*. W.L. Grant, editor. New York: Barnes & Noble, 1967.

Clafin, James. *Lighthouses and Life Saving Along the Massachusetts Coast*. Charleston, SC: Arcadia Publishing, 1998.

Clifford, Barry and Perry, Paul. *Black Ship: The Quest to Recover an English Pirate Ship and Its Lost Treasure*. London: Headline Book Publishing Limited, 1999.

Clifford, Barry and Perry, Paul. *Expedition Whydah: the Story of the World's First Excavation of a Pirate Treasure Ship and the Man Who Found Her*. New York: Harper Collins, 2000.

Conway, Jack. *Head Above Water: Building the Cape Cod Canal*. Baltimore: Publish America, 2005.

Farson, Robert H. *Twelve Men Down: Massachusetts Sea Rescues*. Yarmouth Port, MA: Cape Cod Historical Publications, 2000.

Hathaway, Charles B. *From Highland to Hammerhead: The Coast Guard and Cape Cod*. Chatham, MA: By the author, 2000.

Heath, Dwight B., ed. *Mourt's Relation: A Journal of the Pilgrims at Plymouth*. Cambridge, MA: Applewood Books, 1986.

Johnson, Robert Erwin. *Guardians of the Sea: History of the United States Coast Guard, 1915 – to the Present*. Annapolis, MD: Naval Institute Press, 1987.

Kupperman, Karin Ordahl. *Settling with the Indians: The meeting of English and Indian Cultures in America, 1580-1640*. Totowa, NJ: Rowan & Littlefield, 1980.

Lombard, Percival Hall. *The Aptucxet Trading Post: The First Trading Post of the Plymouth Colony*. Bourne, MA: Bourne Historical Society, 1968.

Peters, Russell. *The Wampanoags of Mashpee*. W. Barnstable, MA: Indian Spiritual and Cultural Training Council, 1987.

Pletcher, larry B. *It Happened on Massachusetts*. Guilford, CT: Globe Pequot Press, 1999.

Schneider, Paul. *The Enduring Shore: A History of Cape Cod, Martha's Vineyard, and Nantucket*. New York: Henry Holt & Company, Inc., 2001.

Sheedy, Jack. *Cape Cod Companion: The History and Mystery of Old Cape Cod*. Barnstable, MA: Harvest Home Books, 1999.

Winslow, Edward. *Good News from New England*. Bedford, MA: Applewood Books, 1996. First Publication in 1624.

Wood, William. *New England's Prospect*. Amherst, MA: University of Massachusetts Press, 1977.

WEBSITES

Archiving Early America *www.earlyamerica.com*

The Barnstable Patriot *www.barnstablepatriot.com*

Bourne Historical Society *www.bournehistoricalsociety.org*

Brewster Chamber of Commerce *www.brewster-capecod.com*

Cape Cod History and Genealogy *www.capecodhistory.us*

Cape Cod Online *www.capecodonline.com*

Cape Cod Museum of Natural History *www.ccmnh.org*

Cranberry Marketing Committee *www.uscranberries.com*

Eastham Historical Society *www.easthamhistoricalsociety.org*

Falmouth Museums on the Green *www.falmouthhistoricalsociety.org*

Historic New England *www.historicnewengland.org*

History Matters *www.historymatters.gmu.edu*

Mass Monuments *www.massmoments.org*

Mayflower History *www.mayflowerhistory.com*

Metro West Dive Club *www.mwdc.org*

Nantucket Historical Association *www.nha.org*

Oceanspray *www.oceanspray.com*

PBS *www.pbs.org*

Pilgrim Hall Museum *www.pilgrimhall.org*

Sandwich Cape Cod *www.sandwichcapecod.com*

Sandwich Glass Museum *www.sandwichglassmuseum.org*

United States Coast Guard *www.uscg.mil*

PHOTO CREDITS

Forward: Gaffney, Walter M. *Map of Cape Cod, Massachusetts.* 1932. Wikipedia *www.wikipedia.org*

Introduction: Cape Cod & the Islands Map, Cape Cod Chamber of Commerce. *www.capecodchamber.org/maps*

Chapter 1: Collier, John. *Hauling in a cod aboard a Portuguese fishing dory off Cape Cod Massachusetts.* 1942. Photograph. Library of Congress. *www.loc.gov*

Chapter 2: Collier, John. *Harvest of a trawl aboard a Portuguese drag boat off Cape Cod Massachusetts.* 1942. Photograph. Library of Congress. *www.loc.gov*

Chapter 3: Currier & Ives. *Landing of the Pilgrims at Plymouth 11th Dec. 1620.* Between 1838–1856. Lithograph, hand colored. Library of Congress. *www.loc.gov*

Chapter 4: Matteson, Tompkins Harrison (painting) & Gauthier (engraving). *The pilgrims signing the compact, on board the May Flower, Nov 11th, 1620.* c1859. Engraving. Library of Congress. *www.loc.gov*

Chapter 5: Boughton, George Henry. *Pilgrims going to church.* 1867. Painting. Library of Congress. *www.loc.gov*

Chapter 6: Reinhart, Charles Stanley. *Lion Gariner in Pequot War.* c1890. Watercolor. Wikimedia Commons. *www.commons.wikimedia.org*

Chapter 7: Kelley, Shawnie. *Aptucxet Trading Post.* 2011. Photograph.

Chapter 8: Unknown. *Exterior – View from Northwest. 1935. - Cape Cod Windmill, Samoset Road, Eastham, Barnstable County, MA.* 1935. Photograph. Library of Congress. *www.loc.gov*

Chapter 9: Buttersworth, Thomas. *A Royal Navy brig chasing and engaging a well-armed pirate lugger.* c1800. Oil on Canvas. Wikipedia. *www.wikipedia.org*

Chapter 10: Rinaldo, Karen. *The Battle of Falmouth / Reenactment 1999.* Oil painting. Falmouth Town Hall Mural. Karen Rinaldo. *www.karenrinaldogallery.com*

Chapter 11: Kelley, Shawnie. *Boat on a Cape Cod marsh.* 2014. Photograph.

Chapter 12: Rothstein, Arthur. *Gathering cranberries that are floating on the surfae of a flooded bog, Burlington County, New Jersey.* Oct 1938. Photograph. Library of Congress. *www.loc.gov*

Chapter 13: Lincoln, E.F. *The Nimrod of Falmouth Mass 1812.* 1919. Painting. Falmouth Historical Society.

Chapter 14: Fischer, Anton Otto. *Chase of the Constitution, July 1812.* Unknown date. Paiting. Wikimedia Commons. *www.commons.wikimedia.org*

Chapter 15: Stubbs, William P. *A merchant brig under shortened sail.* c1880. Oil on Canvas. Wikipedia. *www.wikipedia.org*

Chapter 16: Poole, A.F. *Sandwich Village, Barnstable County, Mass., looking west, 1884.* 1884. Illustration. Library of Congress. *www.loc.gov*

Chapter 17: Charman, Rodney J.K. *The Great Fire of 1846.* 1944. Painting. Egan Maritime Institute. *http://www.eganmaritime.org*

Chapter 18: Kelley, Shawnie. *Captain Edward Penniman House.* 2008. Photograph.

Chapter 19: Historic American Engineering Record (HAER). *INTERIOR, MAIN EQUIPMENT ROOM - French Cable Station, Cove Road & MA Route 28, Orleans, Barnstable County, MA.* 1987. Photograph. Library of Congress. *www.loc.gov*

Chapter 20: The World's Work. *The Wireless Station at South Wellfleet, Massachusetts.* March, 1903, pages 3194-3201. Photograph. United States Early Radio History. *www.earlyradiohistory.us*

Chapter 21: Bain News Service. *Joining of Waters, Cape Cod Canal.* 1914. Photograph. Library of Congress. *www.loc.gov*

Chapter 22: Clockwise from upper left: 1. Boston Post. "Shelled by Submarine off Coast of Cape Cod." July 22, 1918. Photograph. Boston Post. 2. Unknown. Photograph of Perth Amboy Tugboat. Date unknown. Photograph. War History Online. *www.warhistoryonline.com* 3. Unknown. Photograph of German U-Boat SM U-156. Date unknown. Photograph. Will Interpret for Food *www.willinterpretforfood.blogspot.com* 4. Unknown. Photograph of Erie Railroad's Daniel Willard, O&W's Ontario, Lehigh Valley's Perth Amboy and Lackawanna's Scranton at Vineyard Haven, Martha's Vineyard due to ice. Date Unknown. DVRBS.com *www.dvrbs.com*. 5. Unknown. *Lifesavers from U.S. Station No. 40.* Unknown. Photograph. History Press Blog. *www.historypressblog.net*

Chapter 23: US Army Corp of Engineers. *Cape Cod Bourne Bridge and Railroad Bridge*. 1999. Photograph. Wikipedia. *www.wikipedia.org*

Chapter 24: Kelsey, Richard C. *The stern of the tanker Pendleton*. 1952. Photograph. United States Coast Guard. *www.uscg.mil*

Chapter 25: Rosskam, Edwin. *Untitled*. 1940. Photograph. Library of Congress. *www.loc.gov*

Chapter 26: Scott, Theodore. *Whydah-gold*. 2010 Photograph. Wikimedia Commons. *www.commons.wikimedia.org*

Chapter 27: Harris, Rick. *Truro - Highland Light*. 2012. Wikipedia Commons. *www.commons.wikimedia.org*

Chapter 28: Nickerson. *Chase and capture of blackfish*. 1885. Photograph. Library of Congress. *www.loc.gov*

Chapter 29: Rosskam, Edwin. *Untitled*. 1940. Photograph. Library of Congress. *www.loc.gov*

Chapter 29 Cape Cod Chamber of Commerce. Maps: *Upper/Mid Cape Cod, Lower/Mid Cape Cod, Outer Cape Cape, Martha's Vineyard, Nantucket*; *www.capecodchamber.org/maps*

INDEX

Dune Shacks of Peaked Hill Bars 164

E

Eastham 28, 39–43, 47, 56–58, 100–105
Eastham Cove Burying Ground 40
Eastham Historical Society 42
Eastham Windmill 42
Edgartown 4
Edward Gorey House 165
Egan Maritime Institute 96
Elizabeth Islands 7, 9–11, 68
Esther Underwood Johnson Nature Center 148

F

Falmouth 74
Falmouth Artillery Company 68–69
Falmouth Garden Club 70
Falmouth Harbor 53, 69
Falmouth Historical Society 70–71
Field, Cyrus 107–108
Fire Hose Cart House 94
First Congregational Church 96
First Encounter Beach 30–31, 39
Fitzgerald, Captain John 136
Flying Horses Carousel 4
Fortes Beach 164
Fortes, Eugenia 164
Fort Hill 100–102
Fort Mercer 136–141
Fortune 39–40
Freedom Cruise Lines 95
French Cable Station 107, 109–111

G

Gay Head 3
Gay Head Cliffs 7, 164
Gay Head Lighthouse 5
German U-156 126–127
Gorey, Edward 165
Gosnold, Bartholomew 56

Gosnold, Captain Bartholomew 1–4, 7–10, 13, 52
Gosnold's Monument 10
Graveyard of the Atlantic 141, 155
Gray Gables 163
Gray Gables Railroad Station 37
Great Fire 92–94
Great Island 45, 48–49
Great Island Tavern 49
Great Marsh 43
Great Storm of 1978 147
Green Briar Nature Center & Jam Kitchen 162
Gut, the 49

H

Hall, Captain Henry 62
Hallett Barn 70
Hallett, Maria 45–46, 150
Harding Point 143
Harwich 39, 41–42, 62
Harwich Historical Society 65
Harwich Port 59, 142
Hawthorne, Charles 162
Head of the Meadow Beach 148
Herring Cove 148
Higgins, Richard 40
Highland House Museum 158
Highland Light 155–158
Highland Links 157–158
HMS Newcastle 75
HMS Spenser 75
Holbrook, Jesse 156
Hopkins, Giles 40
Hopkins, Stephen 25, 28
Howe Cranberries 62
Howe, Eli 62–63
Howland, John 28, 36
Hoxie House 103–104
Hy–Line Cruises 95

"Traveling Cape Cod is extremely sensory-driven and deeply experiential. Every single visit I become more immersed in my home away from home; discovering something new, something beautiful, something sublime. Sometimes without looking for it and other times, actively seeking out a new experience. It might be a slice of unexpected history, a jaw-dropping sunset, a crazy delicious plate of food, or a staggeringly tall dune. I'll never stop falling in love with Cape Cod!"

Shawnie Kelley has written several books, including *It Happened on Cape Cod* and contributes to a variety of history and food magazines. She is a partner in Wanderlust Tours, specializing in cultural and culinary travel, and teaches travel seminars and cooking classes. Shawnie lives in Columbus, Ohio, but is based in Yarmouth when on the Cape. Her Cape Cod favorites include: low tide at Paines Creek Beach, oyster po'boys in Wellfleet, the Province Land Dunes, and the Nantucket Wine Festival.